INTRODUCTION

Fife, with its diverse a... been strangely neglected in the ... This may perhaps be explained b... in Scotland mainly with mountai... the routes suggested in this b... awareness of the delightful va... gentler countryside. ...p to extend ..., to be found in this

Established walking routes are regrettably few and much energy is expended in their preservation. This is of course essential but it does focus attention on a fixed pattern. Many tracks were originally created for utilitarian purposes, such as access to a church, to work or to a market, whereas the need now is for recreational access. Even where new routes are made they tend to be linear, though circular walks are favoured by the modern car-owning walker. Most of the following walks are devised with this in mind, usually returning to convenient starting points while avoiding busy public roads as much as possible.

Investigating the changes in the routes followed by travellers in and across Fife during the last three centuries, the author has had the good fortune to discover many abandoned tracks through the wilder country of the region and would like to share this experience with others. Since many were abandoned because they were too steep they are found mainly on the upland areas in Fife. For this reason and because it is also contains the most rural landscape there are more walks in the north east district. In the south and west there is the compensating interest of the legacy of the recent industrial past, as will be seen in Walks 1 and 2.

Many walks, already recognised as 'rights of way', have fallen into disuse since the advent of motor vehicles and become overgrown, especially where they were isolated sections. Indeed, they are frequently in danger of closure as the period of disuse extends and arguments for their retention grow weaker. It is to reverse this decay that this admittedly arbitrary selection of fifty walks is offered, for the only real assurance of continued use is the walker's tread, followed up by the regular clearance of the worst affected sections. Thus the walker must be prepared to cross mires, undergrowth and other barriers, always with due consideration for those who make a living from the land. The Country Code is printed below, but for our purposes the most important rules are that stock barriers must be left as we find them, damage to crops must be minimised and disturbance to livestock avoided as much as possible, even if that means making quite a wide detour. Rights of access are less rigidly defined in Scotland than in England. However, in return for greater freedom the walker has no right to expect any particular effort on the part of the land occupier to provide crossing places for fences or to keep a track clear of vegetation, so stout boots and clothing are essential.

There are, however, certain walks which the local authorities have undertaken to maintain and in most cases these will be publicised and provided with signposts. Several town walks, such as those in Culross, extend into open country and a link is now proposed by Dunfermline District between Devilla Forest and Valleyfield past Loch Fitty and via Blairadam Forest to Lochore Meadows Country Park. From there Benarty can be climbed and we are then within easy reach of the Lomond Hills Regional Park, with hundreds of acres of open moorland, in Kirkcaldy and North

East Fife Districts.

The coastal portions of several walks suggested here are already included in a survey of the whole Fife coast, from Kincardine to Newburgh, undertaken by the Wemyss Environmental Education Centre, which has also produced guides to shorter walks in the Kirkcaldy district.

The maps in the fifty walks suggested here are solely for locating them on the relevant Ordnance Survey sheets, which are <u>essential</u> (Nos 58 and 59 north of Dunfermline, 65 and 66 to the south). The navigation instructions at the numbered decision points should be followed with care in the light of commonsense and the state of the ground. A detailed description of some walks is available in the form of nature or historical trails from post offices and information offices. In the lettered observations for the walks below only the barest attempt has been made to record the random interests of the author at a particular time of the year. A dedicated bird watcher, geologist or botanist would notice much more and it is hoped that readers will refer to the publications named in the end notes if they want to enjoy the full potential of the walks.

The author is most grateful for the advice and encouragement of fellow members of the Fife Group of the Ramblers Association but the choice of routes is entirely his own. Finally, it must be said that while several rights of way and alleged rights of way are incorporated in these walks the routes suggested should not be used to assert rights of way. All such questions should be referred to the local authorities concerned whose addresses are given at the end of the notes.

THE COUNTRY CODE
Guard against all risk of fire
Fasten all gates
Keep dogs under proper control
Keep to paths across farmland
Avoid damaging fences, hedges and walls
Leave no litter
Safeguard water supplies
Protect wildlife, wild plants and trees
Go carefully on country roads
Respect the life of the countryside

KEY TO MAPS

O	suggested starting point
▬▬▬▬	public road
+·+·+·+·	railway
▴·▴·▴·▴·	railway (disused)
- - - - - -	suggested walking route
············	alternative route or diversion
▵	summit
•	other feature or structure

Visitors to the mediaeval industrial port of Culross can step into a landscape of more recent industry, now being opened up as a walking area by Dunfermline District Council. We start near the Forth shore and head up a wooded den, to pass through dramatic coal bings, along old railway tracks and across an ironstone field near a former smelter, now a pleasant wilderness.

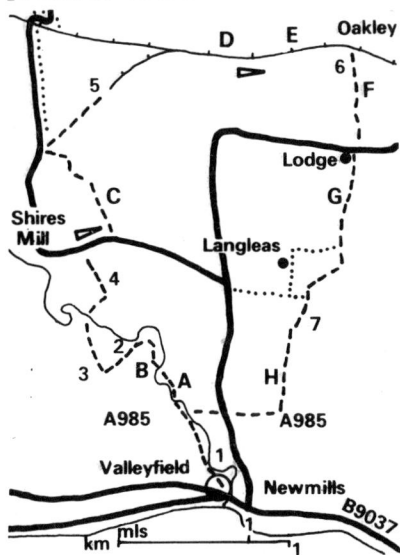

1 GR 011 865. Park on the turning circle by the telephone building between Newmills Bridge and the fork to Culross. Walk north over the red track along the Bluther Burn to beneath the A985 viaduct.

2 Continue through the woods crossing the burn twice. Track swings southwest away from the burn.

3 At edge of wood turn sharp right, walk along the woodland edge to a concrete bridge and head up the slope.

4 Turn left along track under power line to reach public road. Right then left towards overgrown bings now being quarried.

Zigzag track nearly reaches road but turn sharp right and head for screening plant (large tube and hoppers) Check if way ahead clear (alternative route shown).

5 Open ground narrows and approaches the woodland along the Grange Burn, left; the track of a light railway continues, to join the former main line.

6 Before red brick wall on right, turn up slope and cross waste ground. Gate leads onto road. Turn right then left by lodge and down avenue.

7 Preferred route along edge of field ahead and left into wood by gate pillars. At new road (A985) turn right over bridge and return to outgoing path down slope to the right.

A Just north of the viaduct a large black poplar and, after the bridge, a cliff of dark dolerite rock, part of a sill cursed underground by miners. Trees are larch and spruce with bracken, willow, broom, wild raspberries, Saxifraga hirsuta below.

B After the second bridge a large beech and lime. Valleyfield housing appears across field on the left.

C View of the Ochil Hills. Bings of the old Blairhall colliery are now partly covered with scrub, but some material is being rewashed for salvaged coal.

D At two points along the main track thin seams have been dug. Do not approach overhang too closely.

E Much of the railway ballast is blast furnace slag (pale grey and pitted with gas bubbles).

F from the bank see the school, north, on the site of the Forth Iron Company, closed in 1869. The area we are on has been worked for ironstone and used as a dump for waste. Pink centaury, red elder, downy pepperwort.

G The road south of the lodge is mostly blast furnace slag. Remains of a light railway embankment are crossed.

H In ponds: irises, meadowsweet, kingcups.

3

Walk 2 CHARLESTOWN AND LIMEKILNS   6 miles (9.6 km)

Named after the son of the founder, Lord Elgin, Charlestown was built about 1760 to exploit a thick band of limestone, shipped from a new harbour. We can imagine the immense volume of stone removed and view the waggonways which brought coal from near Dunfermline. We then pass through pleasant landscape inland and back by the port of Limekilns.

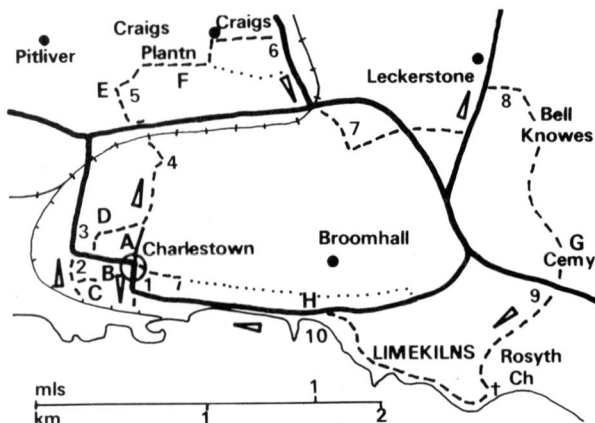

1 GR 066 837. Local guide book available at post office. Walk south to the bend in the road, between the police house and the estate office and then down steps under arch. Turn right.
2 After the last kiln and where the road bears left, turn back right to a fence.

Beyond are the tops of the kilns. To the left, overgrown, is a waggonway. Return towards the road and turn half right up the slope to join the waggonway.
3 By the bus stop enter the woods and examine the West Quarry mine entrances, left (keep an eye on children).
4 Turn right and left to bridge over railway. Down right to cross A985 to footpath. Walk left and turn right to Pitliver
5 Before building, left, turn right into strip of woodland. Where track crosses a break turn north past Craigs farm.
6 Clamber up to the disused tarmac road and follow down to the A985. Cross to go under right hand railway arch.
7 Where woodland begins, turn left and follow ditch round to next wood. Cross ditch into wood, go on to cross the main road and then along field track to next road. Turn left.
8 Down farm road past Leckerstone Cottages and right at end of wood. Turn left at next corner and find way through Bell Knowes copse to south side, arriving at wicket gate. Through gateway to track leading to Douglas Bank cemetery.
9 Cross A985 again and take track to right of Brucehaven farmhouse, over wooded knoll and down path to old church.
10 Take the inland loop of the old main street and look for the King's Cellar, right, before the Post Office.

A Post office is in old granary (hoist door above). Past the south end a deep slot in the rock to drain the East Quarry.
B The incline was part of a ropeway along which laden wagons helped to pull up empty ones.
C The kilns were fed from the top with limestone and coal, the burnt lime or 'shells' being raked out into carts below. Much of it was shipped, but some went by the Shell Road.
D The Charlestown Band of the Limestone Coal Group of strata of the Upper Carboniferous formation has been worked all over southern Fife. It was last worked in 1936. Fossils.
E Pitliver Mill on the left used the water of the Lyne Burn to make linen yarn and later to grind corn.
F A fine view from this ridge of Dunfermline. Broomhall, right, was first built in 1704 and later extended.
G In the centre of the cemetery are the graves of many seamen and airmen; there are Indian, Jewish and Polish names.
H The King's Cellar may have stored imported wine in the 14th century. Note the Pitcairn arms (1581).

This shares with the first walk the legacy of earlier mineral working, but more widely dispersed, over a landscape of grassland and small farmsteads, around the quiet village of Saline. Old coal and ironstone workings are found on the slopes of Saline Hill, a volcanic neck surrounded by lithified ash, and from the summit there are fine views.

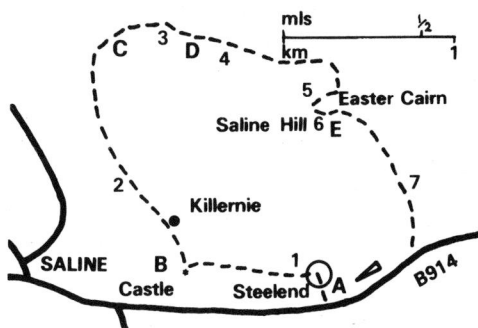

1 GR 041 923. From the shop at Steelend on the B914 walk round the back of the houses and climb gently across the hillside up to the ruin of Killernie Castle. Turn right and pass Killernie steading.
2 Continue along the contour to the left of a decoratively derelict hawthorn hedge to a finger post. Take the track to West Lethans.
3 Just before a beech avenue begins, pass behind a rocky knoll, right. Make uphill to a grassed-over low wall and follow this.
4 After Sheardrum plantation appears on the skyline, right, and where there is a gap in the wall, head for the far left corner of the plantation.
5 Climb the far side of the wood to a cliff, an old volcanic neck. Go round to the right and climb to summit.
6 Walk eastwards till two dykes intersect, cross to the right and head half left gently downhill until you reach a low ridge running directly down the slope with a solitary iron post.
7 Descend in the steps in the turf and follow a larger ridge between small bings. Take track to the main road and turn right to start.

A The housing estate was built for miners at the Bandrum Colliery, opposite.
B Killernie Castle was inhabited in 1592 (dated stone). From here you can see the Wallace monument and Stirling Castle with the Trossachs beyond. The steep wall of the Ochils faces us to the northwest and has the town of Dollar at its foot.
C Ahead on the other side of the valley is the white Hillside House, which stands on the Dunfermline to Rumbling Bridge road, the A 823. This was completed as a new turnpike road in 1810 and was exceptionally well engineered for the time.
D As you climb past the knoll you can see Knock Hill with its radio aerials. The Sunday racing circuit is the other side.
E From the double ramparts of the hill fort we can see Loch Glow in the Cleish Hills, Mossmorran refinery and Edinburgh.

Walk 4 BLAIRADAM FOREST   7 miles (11.3km)

A car may be parked at the junction north of Maryburgh, most
easily accessible from the second Great North Road, now the
B896. The layout of the area managed by the Forestry
Commission is largely that devised by William Adam in the
18th century, and the family still lives in the house. Thus
the access roads were chosen for amenity as well as timber
operations and are bordered by a wide variety of tree
species. At the time of the original plantations the owner
owed much of his prosperity to the several coal mines of
which evidence can still be seen. The transport of coal was
one of the considerations which led the Adams to press for
improvements on the Great North Road.

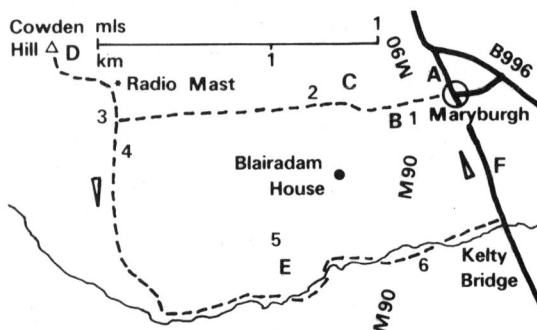

1 GR 137 961. Walk
under the motorway and
climb the slope. On
your left is a walled
garden with cottage.
Continue uphill
leaving North Blair
House on your left to
reach the edge of the
forest by the gas
pipeline marker.
2 Take the centre
track which winds
uphill; at next fork
bear left. At cross roads turn right to pass radio mast.
3 Follow this road round to Cowden Hill, through gate.
4 Descend and retrace steps as far as the cross roads and go
straight on. Ignore tracks tothe left which lead to private
ground and walk downhill to Pieries Burn Bridge. Do not cross
but turn left. Take grassy track parallel to the burn.
5 At the bed of the mineral railway turn left to visit old
mine buildings and return. Scramble down left to a burnside
track. The tumbled abutments of a railway bridge can be seen.
Pass over two bridges and at the T junction turn right. This
shortly meets a complex junction, but head for the tunnel
below the motorway.
6 Pass Dullomuir Farm on your left and reach the 18th century
road north of Kelty Bridge. Walk north to start.

A The track to the north is the unimproved part of the 18th
century road which ran south, up hill and down dale, past
Kirk of Beath to Queensferry. It was replaced by a new road
under an Act of 1809 with easier gradients, still used by
more leisurely and local traffic.
B In the walled garden are experiments in establishing
traditional wild flowers and in tree nursery techniques. The
two holm oaks (Ilex) may be from the original planting.
C North Blair has two great venetian windows on east and
south sides. Blairadam House can be seen through the park
beeches to the left. Formerly a factor's house it owes little
of its external appearance to the two famous architect sons,
but has a handsome simplicity. To the right Loch Leven comes
into view.
D The summit is formed of dolerite with marked prismatic
jointing. You can see the hill reached by the Vane Farm
nature trail southeast of the Loch, on the left of Benarty
Hill. A great sweep of country includes the Grampians, the
Ochils, Knock Hill near Saline and the Pentlands.
E A diversion north here will confirm the past importance of
coal mining to the Blairadam estate.
F Note the marriage lintel '1722' erected when this was the
road to Inverness, far too hilly for later traffic.

6

Archaeological and nature trails are provided by the Fife Ranger Service at the Centre. A differently shaped loch was drained in the 1790s, and the present outline is the result of mining subsidence and subsequent landscaping. The Mary Pit, of which the winding gear frame has been preserved, closed in the 1930s and recently the bings have been levelled. The route climbs through woodland recently acquired by Fife Region, and continues through forest and moor to a superb viewpoint overlooking Loch Leven.

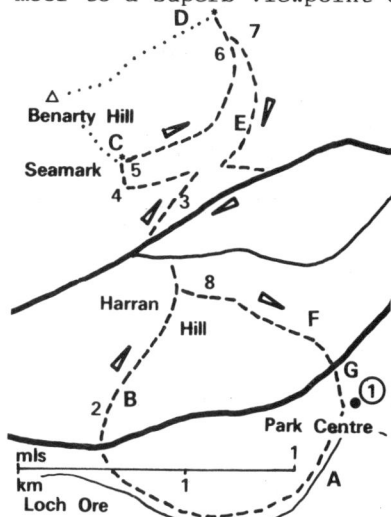

1 GR 171 961. Follow the shore round to meet the rough road. Turn left and enter the signposted Harran Hill Wood.
2 Turn up left into wood at large boulder, follow track to top road and turn left onto the Ballingry road. Turn right. After 50 yards, at a layby, follow a grassy wheeltrack climbing gently through the wood.
3 Going becomes difficult after coming to field fence, so follow field side till you come to a forest road. Turn left.
4 At the end of a clear felled area climb a bank, right, and follow a narrow steep track directly uphill until you reach a stone wall with heather beyond.
5 The stone base of a seamark is to be found on a knoll to the north. Follow the edge of the wood to a sharp bend in the wall. Go downhill to meet a grassy forest track to the left. Aim for two sycamores on the skyline.
6 Near the end of the horizontal track follow a footpath up to the left through the trees and emerge where a ladder stile can be seen on the crest of the ridge. You should go no further since between you and Loch Leven is the Vane Farm nature reserve. Return to the forest track.
7 Continue past a sharp bend down to the right along a rough road. When the field is reached you can return more easily by turning left, meeting the Ballingry road further to the east, and then turn right.
8 In Harran Hill Wood an alternative exit leads to a path across the hill and you descend directly towards the Mary Pit winding gear.

A The Centre's guide mentions grebe, tufted duck and pochard.
B The wood consists largely of oak and beech.
C Old tall heather in places, so keep to the tracks as all heather can quickly die out under foot traffic.
D A separate visit to the RSPB reserve is recommended. A trail leads from the centre to a viewpoint on Vane Hill.
E Where the track is directly above a square wood on the bottom road, there is in a small rock face on your right a splendid example of 'onion weathering' of dolerite.
F The hillside here shows the ridge and furrow strips of the communal fermtoun type of cultivation.
G You may well meet a retired miner who worked in the Mary Pit. Much of the housing in nearby Ballingry was provided for the workforce.

Walk 6 CULLALOE HILLS AND OLD NORTH ROAD 6.2 miles (10 km)

A massive outcrop of the great dolerite sill forms this chain of low hills, now crowned with woodland, and the rock structure can be seen in an active quarry. The return route takes in the switchback ´Old North Road´ from Burntisland towards Perth; a dramatic landscape with good views across the Forth.

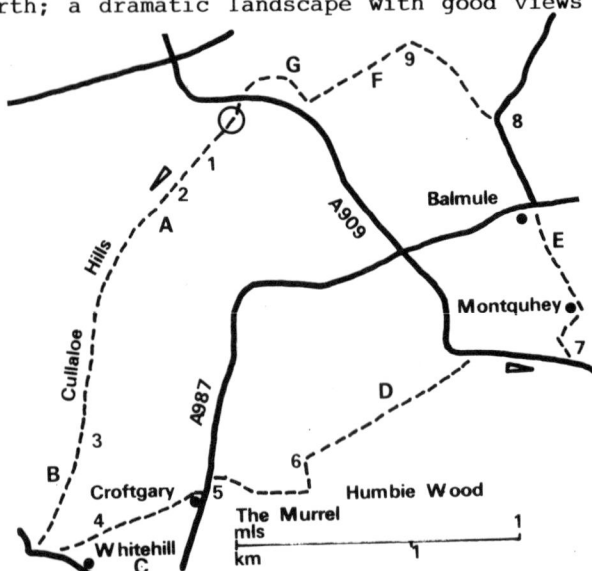

1 GR 187 889. Park in the open area and walk along track.
2 Left of radio mast and of stone temple beyond. Bear left.
3 At the triangular intersection turn left along a new track with quarry chippings. Continue past quarry and down to road Turn left and left again at the transformer inside railings.
4 Through the gate and follow the lower edge of the field. Cross corner to gate. Here footpath needs clearing, so walk along field edge till next gate. Through Croftgary steading to road.
5 Turn left and right to The Murrel. Left at next T junction
6 Turn right through gate between lime trees. Follow track cut out of hillside to the A 909. Turn right onto road.
7 Turn left at water works sign, bear right at cottages
8 Where cottage stands on sharp right corner, turn left between hedges. Continue at side of grass field between derelict hawthorns.
9 Path ahead overgrown. Enter field to the left and keep along fence till cleared section accessible near brick viaduct. Turn right and follow curve to main road. Turn left and right to start.

A The great roof slabs of the temple are almost indestructible but the small elm is having a good try.
B At quarry rim note the great vertical joints of the sill.
C The building at the crossroads on the right is a toll-house erected in 1807 on a new road from Kirkcaldy.
D Ahead the craggy knoll of Dunearn broods over the Stenhouse Reservoir. Summit has hut circles and a fort.
E You are now on the ´Old North Road´, superseded after 1810 by what is now the A 909. The natural surface is worn through to bare rock in places but has been built up with large stones on the steep sections.
F Built up between ditches like a Roman road, this section avoided the quagmire which the old road had become.
G A now disused road swings round to the north and west. Broken through by a pipeline (see posts), it has been carefully restored. Earlier marker stones at regular intervals are a reminder of how such a road could become unidentifiable in winter.

Walk 7   THE BINN AND DUNEARN   6 miles (9.6km)

This combines an exploration of past local industries with magnificent views over the Forth and particularly of the port of Burntisland. Parts are steep and care should be taken of children along the cliff top.

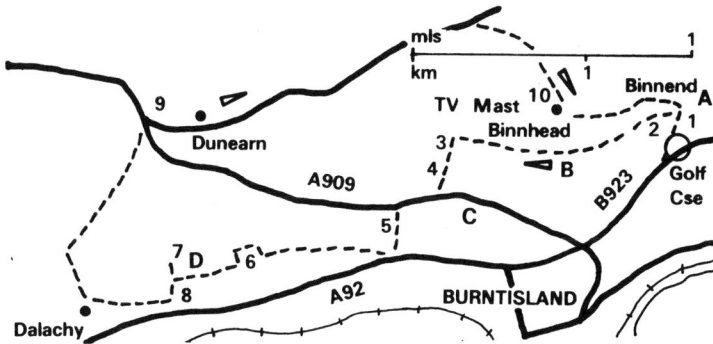

1 GR 241 870. A car may be left on the grass verge opposite the golf clubhouse. Track goes up through woods to opening in a wall.

2 Keep inside fence along the ridge and use the stiles.

3 Descend along edge of wood to gate on left, opposite track from right. A well marked path leads across field.

4 Steep path through wood to road; cross with care to footpath and turn right till end of farm buildings. Turn left down rough track, electricity station on your right, followed after zigzags by round concrete water tank.

5 Straight down road to bus shelter on main road. Turn right.

6 At Newbigging the usual route lies to the right of the white lodge, between gate pillars, but the owner would prefer walkers to go further to the right, round the back of the house, and rejoin the original line.

7 Step aside to peep at the underground workings for limestone and the open quarry above for sandstone.

8 Look for ivy covered gate on right and step over gap in wall to the Dalachy road. Turn right up the brae at Dalachy.

9 Cross A909 and walk along ridge road past second belt of trees to a metal gate with a small swing gate beside. Follow wall to hollow way. Top of the bank on the right may be easier. Coming out of wood, head left to gate at corner of field, to right of TV mast.

10 Turn right to derelict farmstead, then left. The farm track is too overgrown, so make way along ridge to right of it as far as a small brick wall in the corner. Turn right beyond and pass through deserted village to head of path.

A Despite efforts by the aluminium company, who dump bauxite residues in the old oil shale workings, motor cycle scramblers find this a challenging practice ground.

B The Binn is a mass of coarse volcanic material from nearby vents, interbedded with sandstone bands. The weathered crags below the cliff carry their own flora but should be viewed from a distance. In 1850 the first railway waggons were rolled down ramps from the train ferry onto the far section of the harbour, some to continue their journey to Tayport.

C Through the trees see the old Grange Distillery, last operated in 1920. Passing the farm note the lozenge pillars.

D The Burdiehouse Limestone band was worked after 1946 and the stone was originally exported through the little harbour of Starleyburn. The overlying sandstone was used for Gothenburg Cathedral and a part of Edinburgh University.

A good long hike, but less strenuous than the climb from the
Loch Leven side. The view gradually unfolds and the panorama
from the crest is spectacular. The absence of people makes
it an ideal place for reservoirs. At one, Harperleas, work
is under way to increase capacity by raising the dams. The
top of Bishop Hill has been much quarried for limestone and
fossils may be found. Do not be surprised to see gliders
overhead, for the currents deflected by the west facing
slope provide powerful uplift for the Portmoak club.

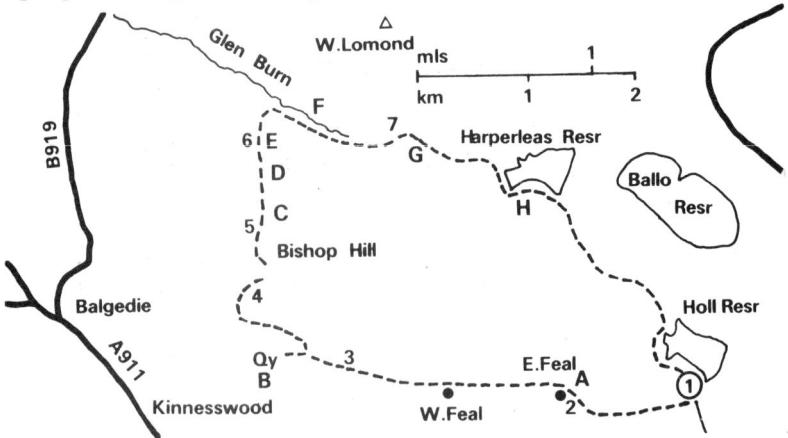

1 GR 225 034. Park on verge on left, beyond end of dam.
Return to crossroads and turn right to West Feal at the park
sign.
2 Go round right hand side of farmstead, through gate.
3 Past the youngest plantation, follow wheel tracks in grass
Diversion: Left into old quarries for fossils and return to
main track. Towards crest of hill and through gateway in
wall, then left, keeping second wall on your right.
4 Where two walls meet, pass through gate and climb knoll
with cairn on the summit. On descent follow landrover track.
5 Track ends at wire fence over low wall. Cross here and
follow grassed over ridge (old wall).
6 Best to descend by wall to gates by the burn. Turn right.
7 Where the track fades out against a wall, climb over and
head along low ridge for blue gate by corner of wood. Follow
forest track. Continue beyond wood back to start.

A East Feal farm was in ruins before Glenrothes was built.
The recent wooden stables signal a reverse trend.
B This is the same geological level as the limestone at
Charlestown (Walk 2). Stems of sea lilies (starfish on
stalks), brachiopods (lamp shells), corals and trilobites.
C Yellow painted boulder on right is marker for pilots.
D Down below on the left is Glenlomond Hospital. Several
steep chutes in hillside here, from moving stone downhill.
E Note contrast between the ´white´ moor on the steep slope,
with its blueberry and pale tussocks, and improved grazing.
Shows up against heather on other side of Glen Burn.
F The deep caves weathered in the sandstone cliff include
one with a pillar at the entrance, ´John Knox´s Pulpit´.
G Patches of sedge on sphagnum moss over black peat.
Weathers better than underlying sand (cornice by path).
H Raised water level would flood forest but for new wire
mesh filled with stones.

Both the West and East Lomond peaks are volcanic necks piercing a sheet of dolerite, which in its turn protects limestone and coal seams. Overgrown quarries are found on the north side and on the slight southern dip are several reservoirs. Patches of poor drainage provide interesting lochs and mosses, with extensive heather where it is drier to the west. The summit is just outwith Fife, but provides perhaps the best point from which to survey the county.

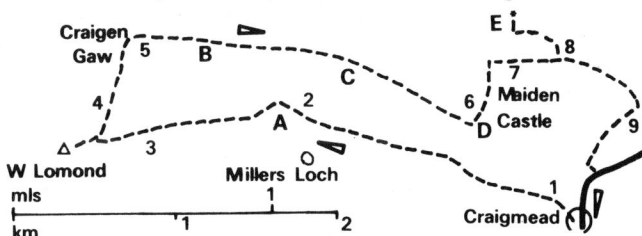

1 GR 227 064. Leave Craigmead by stile and join ridge track.
2 A long wall appears from the left across the end of Miller's Loch. Go round the corner to the right.
3 The quarry to the left of the track is a good shelter for a snack before climbing the zigzag track to the summit.
4 Cross the white moor to the north to reach a gulley. To the right is safe enough, but along a very steep slope, so anyone subject to vertigo may wish to return via the ridge.
5 If going on, scramble down along the burn and where the gulley widens out, take a sheep track to the right. After crossing a burn aim to the left of the crags. At a row of screens or butts for shooters you will see Maiden Castle ahead, reached across some rough grazing.
6 After the Castle, head for a round topped rise to the northeast, away from the main ridge. Over this you will see a sharp corner of woodland beyond. Follow ride down, right.
7 Where the track crosses a firebreak, with a fence against the skyline, right, you can turn left and view the monument.
8 On reaching a circular space from which four forest roads radiate, take the one to the left to visit the monument. Return and go through tunnel of spruce to a field gate.
9 Turn right at the gate to the far end of a fence across the field and then along the woodland edge until just before the point where the burn enters. A tumbled wall by a rowan leads to a firebreak up to the road. Turn right to Craigmead

A Note the commonty boundary stones, one marked 'WM'. This is the largest area of common grazing in Fife.
B The quarries were working the basal limestone of the Carboniferous Limestone Series. Between this and the the next band up, worked near the East Lomond, the massive sill of dolerite was injected, seen in Craigen Gaw.
C Since this is a regional park, grouse shooting has almost ceased.
D It is suggested that the isolated knoll would have been surrounded by marsh, and that other lines of defence existed higher up the flanks. The gateway at the eastern end was approached by a ramp across the ditch.
E This remarkable structure, reminiscent of a lighthouse, was erected in 1855, as the tablet states, to honour the planter of these extensive woodlands.

The East Lomond is a remnant of a volcanic neck piercing the overall sill of dolerite which forms the main ridge. From its summit most parts of Fife can be identified, and the route down past Falkland House takes us to a spectacular wooded den with a waterfall you can walk beneath. On our return we visit one of the highest limestone kilns in Fife.

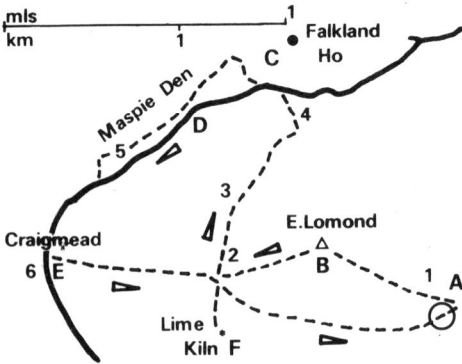

1 GR 253 057. The path from the car park to the summit is clearly defined; on descending to the west, head for a point in line with the far Ballo Reservoir where two walls converge by two small trees on the main track.

2 At wicket gate by country park sign, turn right along the left side of a series of shallow overgrown quarries. After last quarry, head across patch of white (grass) moor with heather on your left. Make for grass strip and you should see the squat tower of the Bruce monument in woodland ahead. Where grass track broadens, veer round to right along contour to wall with posts at intervals.

3 Cross wall by tree and head for nearest corner of pine wood at about the same level on the right. Join a sunken path by a line of stones and curve round to the left hand edge of the wood and through it to a stile in a plantation fence. Over this and turn right along inside of fence.

4 At vehicle track turn left and at public road turn left again. After a few yards take a gravel track leading to the right. You will see Falkland House through a gap in a wall on your right. After you cross a stone bridge, turn along a narrow path up and along the Maspie Burn.

5 At the overhanging waterfall at the top of the path, walk under and climb far bank up two pairs of steps. Then sharp turn left and climb up through trees to a field wall. Turn left and follow the side of the wood to a cross fence. After another 30 yards, at a gap in the trees, follow grassy path across the burn and up to main road. Turn right.

6 At Craigmead car park turn left along main ridge track back to start, visiting the lime kiln from the sign.

A A country park map on a board can be viewed by the road between the radio installation and the toilets.

B An orientation table on the summit points out the principal features in the landscape.

C Falkland House was built by Mr O.T.Bruce in 1839 after his marriage to Miss Bruce of Falkland. It shows a return to a Jacobean style, embellished with domed Scottish turrets.

D In the Den you will see a small waterfall formed by a hard band of dolerite, the same rock as the massive slab which caps the Lomond ridge. Among the less usual trees are the noble fir and the western red cedar.

E Opposite Craigmead car park the dolerite rock whose joints have been weathered almost into spheres.

F Alternate charges of limestone and coal were fed into the top of the kiln and after burning, the lime was raked out through the arch at the bottom.

On the edge of Glenrothes, we start from the headquarters of the new town, an 18th century mansion, set in a beautiful park and with many specimen and exotic trees. The outbuildings house craft workshops to which you are invited. The walk passes the edge of the old town of Markinch with its 16th century church on a hill, and follows a direct route to the dispersed village of Star. There are wide views from Cuinin Hill and the walk is notable for the variety of types of woodland encountered.

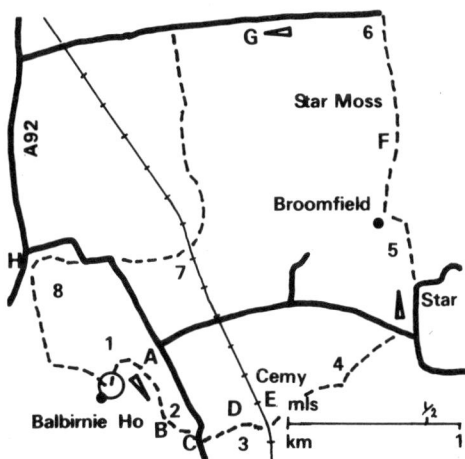

1 GR 290 025. Pass the golf clubhouse which you will leave on your right, and walk along the burn, crossing to the far bank by a bridge and back again where there is a ford for riders.

2 Go along path round field to East Lodge on the road. Turn right and then left through a gap in the opposite wall. Climb bank to the ridge of Markinch Hill.

3 At end of ridge continue round to the right until you can descend on grass to lower path. Pass through barrier onto road and under railway arch. Climb path right of cemetery.

4 After gap in wall, left, climb steps to path over wooded hill. At far end walk to highest point of field for view.

5 After entrance sign to Star, bear left for Broomfield Farm.

6 Turn left at T junction and walk to beginning of of a large pine wood on your left. Take the first ride through the wood and bear right after a large ditch.

7 Follow track over railway and onto public road. Re-enter Balbirnie Park over gate, follow gravel and woodchip pony track to the right round young plantation.

8 On emerging at north drive to house, turn left to start.

A In 1826 when Balbirnie House was rebuilt, the Balfours owned several coalmines, linen mills and ironworks. Exotic trees were later planted and Fir Hill is now crowned by monkey puzzles.

B A notice warning of subsidence is a reminder of the coal workings beneath you.

C the origin of the Stob Cross is obscure but it is reputed to be one of the few sanctuary crosses in Scotland.

D The slope to the north is broken by two levels of terrace. The field beyond has always been known as 'The Playfield',

E The graveyard has a fine collection of well kept yews and makes a curious landmark for inter-city travellers.

F A causeway existed across the Moss before the 18th century and its use as a detour by those wishing to avoid payment of tolls at the New Inn turnpike was a source of sorrow for the trustees who were at pains to close it.

G A group of trees in the field to the north includes the remains of Kirkforthar Chapel

H The circle of stones encloses a group of cists described on the adjacent plaque.

Up on the East Neuk ridge overlooking the Howe with views across to the Lomonds and south towards Markinch. A varied walk with several areas of woodland, relics of coalmining and historic buildings.

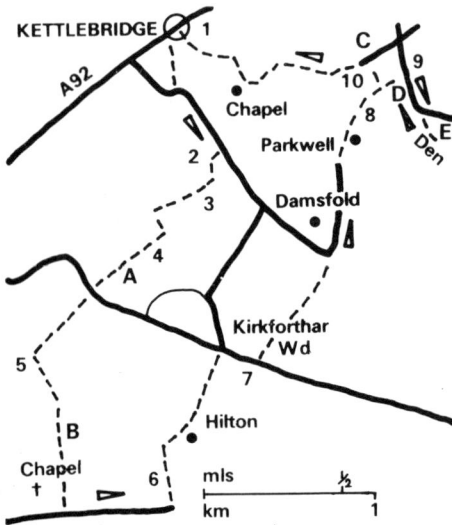

1 GR 307 074. A car can be left in a side road (clear of the bus stop). Through a wicket gate to path along east side of burn, crossed by a footbridge. Up onto track above stone bridge and left.

2 Turn right, down into large hollow across the motor cycle scrambling tracks, round left to cross burn by high bridge.

3 At top of slope turn along field fence to the right as far as corner, then left along old hedge line. Path up the bank overgrown so go past the metal gate and make way through the tussocky grass to the top.

4 At the top of the bank follow the upper edge of the scrub to the road and continue in the same line on the other side.

5 You will have to turn left along a further scrubby strip till you can see the upper end of a row of beech trees down northern slope. Follow these to lower road and turn left.

6 Follow in or alongside the sunken track up past the farm.

7 At the main road turn right and after 200 yards follow grassy strip through the trees on your left. Across the more defined woodland path and continue to northern edge of wood. In the same line a strip of ground ahead between fences appears blocked by broom, but is only for a few yards.

8 Track becomes grassy strip. Aim for derelict buildings. A sunken way lies to the right but keep above it. A broom filled hollow way opposite is just negotiable.

9 At the main road turn right past a paddock, and where the road turns left look for a large round fence post set back from verge. Follow track down and round to left into den.

10 Take kirk road and where it crosses farm road turn left and follow road down past Chapel Farm to the start.

A Below you the old Forthar limeworks are largely filled in, but they were the principal source of agricultural lime for northern Fife in the late 18th century. Much of the coal used to burn limestone came from along the Kirkcaldy road,

B Note ruins of Kirkforthar House, with dovecot and chapel.

C The kirk road points straight towards Kettle Church and is a right of way supported by custom rather than usage.

D In the ground behind the paddock can be seen circular banks marking the positions of bottle pits, each developed to the limits of safety. The channel could be a canal.

E Near the burn a vertical rock face has a square socket, possibly to secure apparatus over the shaft nearby.

This takes us into some of the wildest places on the Rigging -- the spine of the East Neuk. Part of the old Edinburgh to St Andrews road is followed and there are extensive views over the Forth and towards the Highlands.

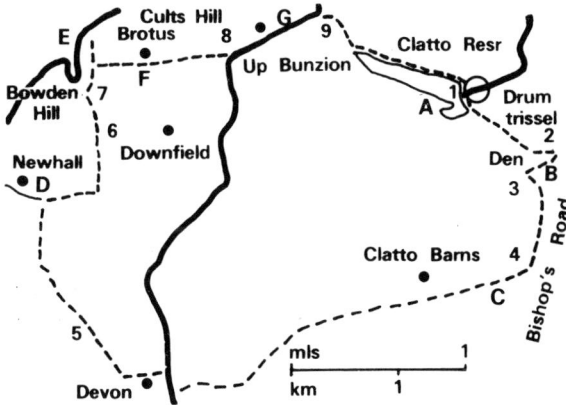

1 GR 366 078. Pass between the large building and the overspill channel; walk along the dam from the right. Cross channel by low weir. At the start of the second dam, scramble up left to small gate and follow field side of fence.

2 Twenty yards before end of fence, climb fixed gate and descend, right, to fence corner and wooden bridge.

3 Climb sunken way up left through trees and thence to gate in wall. Turn right and through two small gates.

4 Leave fence line to follow field walls and join farm road.

5 At foot of slope: through the right hand metal gate and straight on along grassy strip.

6 After road turns towards Downfield, head for gate on right of fence line and follow east side of burn. If impracticable, keep left of wall, pass along narrow field and over burn before wooded den.

7 Through small gate and turn right to top of spoil heap. You will see the roof of Brotus, but first follow old quarry track straight on to viewpoint and return.

8 Another diversion to viewpoint here.

9 Make way down left side of block of trees and return to start along north bank of reservoir, normally kept open for anglers.

A Amphibious persicary and water crowfoot in flower June. Rock rose between dams and orchids, ragged robin across far dam.

B The zigzag down to the Clatto Burn to ease the gradient breaks the almost straight line of the old Ceres to Kennoway road.

C You are on a 'consumption dyke' -- a neat way of getting rid of field stones. The old road you have left is now the other side of the round topped wood and ran close to the ruined farm on your left, Wester Kilmux. Soon there is a clear view of Largo Law (Walk 16).

D Track to the left leads to a scattered collection of colliers' houses round Coaltown of Burnturk. Coal was often found within a few yards of the Cults Hill limestone it was required to burn.

E A level platform here gives good views over the Howe of Fife. Bowden Hill, left, has ramparts of a hill fort. To the right much of the escarpment has been quarried for limestone. The shale overburden goes to Methil to make Wemyss bricks.

F You might still see a reaper and binder machine near the granary steps at Brotus.

G Continuing the line of the modern road is an abandoned road to Skelpie Farm, part of a former ridge way.

After exploring the wooded den with its ochre mine, deer enclosure and nature trail, the walk takes us up to the edge of the wild ridge country, encounters the Bishop´s Road and returns with views over the Forth.

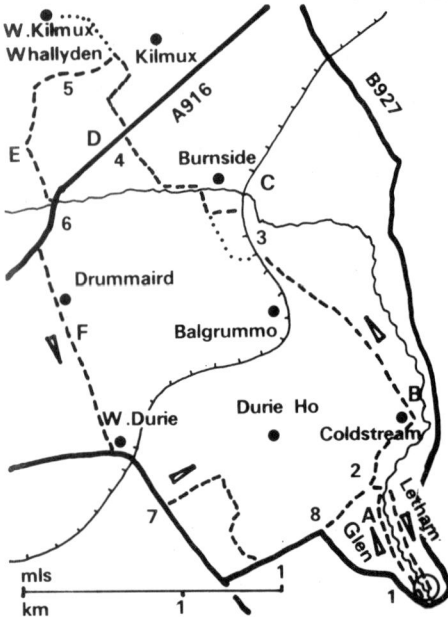

1 GR 382 018. To follow the numbered posts a guide is provided at the visitor centre (green building). The walk leads up the west side of the burn to a bridge. We leave the den, returning on the other side.

2 Take the sloping path up to the left through the gate pillars and turn right along a rough road.

3 Climb railway embankment and walk along to the end. If crops may be damaged, turn left along hedge to other track. Otherwise walk straight on and turn left into road.

4 Turn right at main road A916 and then left at ´Kilmux´. The uphill road ends at the ruined Wester Kilmux farm, but our route lies to the left, along the foot of a low scrub covered slope.

5 Through gate into field and follow round upper edge. At end of fence turn right and follow fence to second large tree. Climb over and cross burn to front of wooden tractor shed.Turn left at white cottage and walk downhill.

6 Cross road bridge and take second turning, past cottages.

7 Turn off main road opposite cottage between stone pillars. Follow road through second gateway and turn right after belt of larch. You pass a walled garden on your left and the modernised Dury Garden Cottage by a gravel track. Turn left where drive meets tarmac road.

8 At ´Buses Only´ area go straight on. You will see the pillars at the top of Letham Glen at the end of the track. Descend to footbridge and return to start down eastern path.

A The vertical cliffs, like those of Balcarres Den (Walk 19), show the effect of rapid downcutting by streams during the recovery from the post-glacial rise in sea level. It was among these shales that the coal and ochre seams were found.

B West Highland cattle may be seen here.

C This railway was planned to run to St Andrews, but only got as far as Lochty (Walk 21).

D The building, left, housed a colliery winding engine.

E The exact line of the old Kennoway to Ceres road by Wester Kilmux is debatable, but it passed through Whallyden and across what is now a field. The road beyond continues the line to the A916.

F Good views of Leven, Methil and across the Forth.

From Lower to Upper Largo and to a beautiful wooded den; through open farmland along an ancient route. Returning by mature woodland and along the coast to the harbour. Lundin Links are typical of the dunes on which the game of golf developed and the old railway is a reminder of the former growth of Largo as a holiday resort.

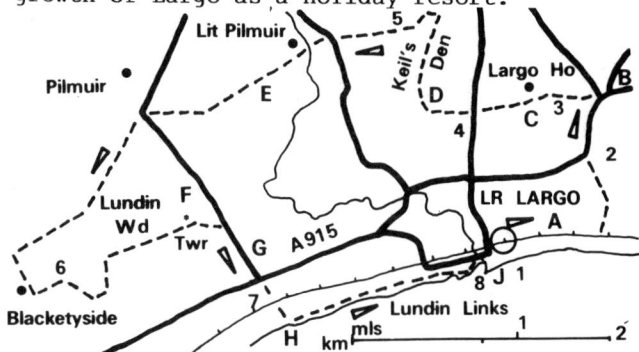

Lit Pilmuir   5   Keil's Den   Largo Ho   B
Pilmuir   E   D   Largo Ho
4   C   3
2
Lundin   F   LR LARGO
Wd   Twr   G   A915   A
6   8   J   1
Blacketyside   7   Lundin Links   1   2
H   km   mls

1 GR 419 026. Car park east of old railway viaduct. Walk along track and over a road cutting by steps, across a small den, then left past a stone wall.
2 Cross to the footpath, round to the turn to Upper Largo church. Keep to left of church and go between gate pillars.
3 Through field gate and round south of ruined Largo House. Keeping the caravan site on the left, turn left at road.
4 Over gate opposite entrance to caravans and along a rather soggy strip to reach the den. Take lower path to footbridge.
5 A small gate leads to a poorly defined path across a field to the next road. Through Little Pilmuir Farm to open track a long slope. All arable here, so detour to be considered.
6 After reaching Blacketyside Farm and turning left to enter strip of woodland, avoid turnings to left till T junction with a marshy place beyond. Past Lundin Tower and three gates to Pilmuir Road, then right.
7 Where Links Road turns left, bear right to old railway bridge and across course. Walk along shore till clubhouse fence, when you can continue at either of two levels. However, when you come to houses you must take the street if the tide is in. Otherwise, climb up old slipway in harbour.
8 Reach car park by passage to right of the Railway Inn.

A Just before a lower car park appears you pass Cardy House and below it the three roofed net factory and flagstaff, all erected by a descendant of Alexander Selkirk. The museum lies to the right. You will have noted the Crusoe Hotel.
B As you turn off the main road note the Wood Hospital on your right backed by Largo Law. Erected in 1665 by a descendant of Admiral Sir Andrew Wood and rebuilt in 1830.
C Largo House by Robert Adam was built in 1750 (over front entrance) by Mr James Durham. After quartering troops in the last war the roof was removed to save rates.
D Keil´s Den is particularly attractive on Spring days since it points south and is sheltered from the prevailing winds.
E This path along the contour gives views of Largo Law and the golf course at Lundin Links, Shell Bay and Kincraig Pt.
F Lundin Tower is a remnant of a house removed in 1876 and a replacement of a 15th century structure. Beyond is a doocot with Gothic windows and chimneys, once the chapel.
G You can see the three red sandstone monoliths of Lundin, remains of a circle, possibly astronomical, pre 1,000 B.C. To view, check with ladies´ golf clubhouse.
H The sandy shore and its backing dunes sweep round to mouth of Leven. To east irregular masses of volcanic rock, banded sandstones streaked by plant debris and oxides of iron.
J Beneath railway viaduct a pair of millstones in front of a modern group of houses in traditional style on the site of a former mill.

Walk 16   LARGO LAW AND UPPER KEIL´S DEN   7 miles (11.3 km)

Exploring the wilder end of the den, we continue past Pitcruvie Castle and climb the Law from the west. On a good day the views are magnificent. We return down to the coast by the attractive lane past Coates and back through Upper Largo.

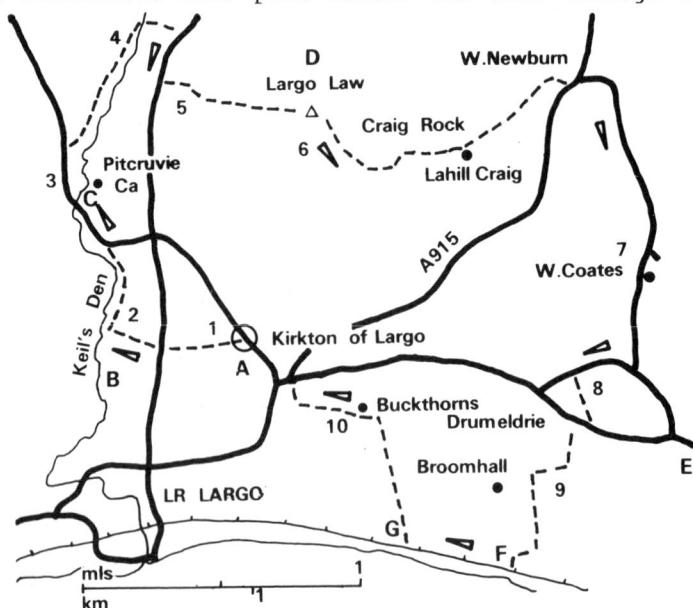

1 GR 422 037. Start by entrance to cemetery. Go west along north side of wall to road and south side beyond.
2 In Keil´s Den keep to top of steep bank. At the road you can stay inside the fence until the bridge.
3 Walk up road to end of woodland on the right and follow upper edge above the burn. Lower paths now badly overgrown.
4 At corner of field continue to right of quarry to reach stone footbridge and walk up to road.
5 Up entrance to Hill House and straight up hillside to wicket gate in fence below strip of trees and climb the Law.
6 Descend in direction of corner of wood below cottages; skirt field to reach track past them and then to A915.
7 Fork right past West Coates Farm buildings.
8 Left after market garden, along high hedge to coast road. Right then left between cottages at Drumeldrie.
9 Follow zigzag farm track down to the shore and walk old railway line to ruined buildings. Turn up right here and follow straight track to Buckthorns Farm steading.
10 Pass to left in front of main buildings and along field wall to row of cottages ´South Feus´. Turn right and cross A915. Turn left at Wood´s Hospital, then right to the start.

A Between the tower with the conical roof and the parish church a retired admiral, Sir Andrew Wood (died 1521), is said to have had a canal dug by English prisoners, who rowed him to church each Sunday. A trough can be detected from the gate below the cemetery.
B The Den is described in Walk 14, and results from rapid downcutting during rise of the post-glacial land surface.
C Pitcruvie Castle with its massive keep existed before 1400. Owner tried by James IV for supporting James III.
D Both summits owe their eminence to the hardness of the rocks of a volcano´s throat.
E A diversion to the old Newburn Church GR 453 036. is worthwhile.Second church at GR 443 035. is now a private residence, as is the schoolhouse.
F Several fish traps can usually be seen along the low tide mark. The building by the burn was a water-powered cornmill.
G Viewforth, the ruined building was part of a saltpan site.

Walk 17 ELIE, SHELL BAY AND ST FORD   8 miles (12.9 km)

We explore three headlands of volcanic rock, one of which
has well marked raised beaches and spectacular columns, and
turn inland to pass through forestry and farmland back to
Elie harbour.

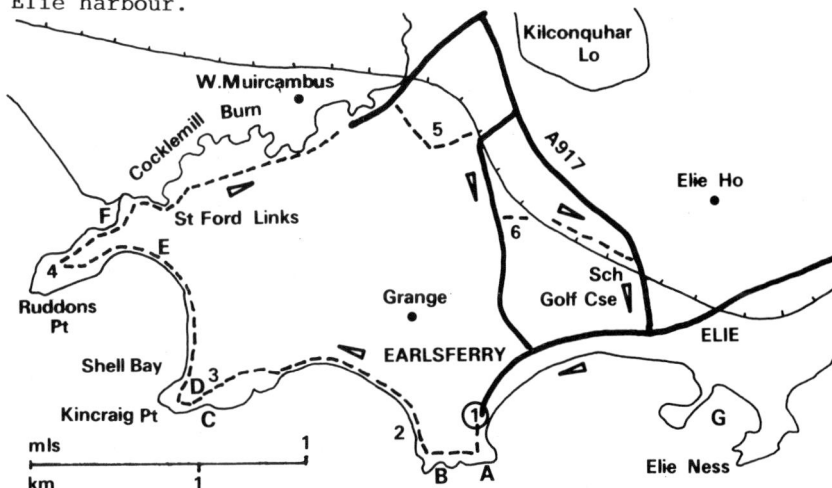

1 GR 481 998. Follow the shore road to the end and then the
footpath round the headland. Good view of bay from knoll.
2 Walk along shore to end of golf course. Kincraig Point can
be explored by the agile at low tide by a route over the
rocks using chains fixed at intervals, but most of us will
prefer to climb the zigzag path to the top of the headland
from which the columns may be viewed.
3 The descent westwards takes us down three abrupt changes
of slope -- the raised beaches, and we follow the green
volcanic rocky shore to the sands of Shell Bay.
4 A small observation point for a former firing range is
worth climbing, then skirt the first belt of trees till the
first gap,left, passing between the fence and the contorted
meanders of the Cocklemill Burn. The forest ride can be
followed till the entrance road to the caravan site, then
turn right at a wooden barrier into another wood.
5 Cross to track to right of building and along to road.
6 Along burn to north edge of wood and follow round
alongside old railway, through the golf course to the A917.
Turn south and find your way to the harbour, where a
diversion can be made to Elie Ness. Round harbour to start.

A A small creek makes a mooring for boats and the columns of
rock have been worn to black shiny surfaces.
B The grassed over bay is a low level raised beach.
C The columns result from the contraction after injected
molten rock has cooled. Joints form parallel to vertical
axes and are seen as polygons in horizontal section.
D The land was depressed by the weight of the ice sheets.
When they melted, over 10,000 years ago the land recovered
by stages marked by these old shorelines, which, as raised
beaches, can be traced at intervals all round Fife.
E On the rough ground of the golf course grow cowslips; on
the path at the edge of the dunes viper´s bugloss, greater
knapweed and many other flowers.
F Longshore drift of sand has all but blocked the Cocklemill
Burn and an area of saltmarsh has developed.
G At the harbour note the old granary and visit Elie Ness
with its coastguard lookout and The Lady´s Tower, the latter
an 18th century summer house for Lady Anstruther to bathe,
when a bell was rung in the town. Around the Ness the dark
greenish rocks have no regular layers and are a jumble of
volcanic debris containing rocks of diverse origin.

19

Walk 18   ST MONANCE AND KILCONQUHAR   8.5 miles   (13.6 km)

Some rough coastal walking with a few scrambles, then through farmland to view Kilconquhar Loch and village returning down the St Monance Burn.

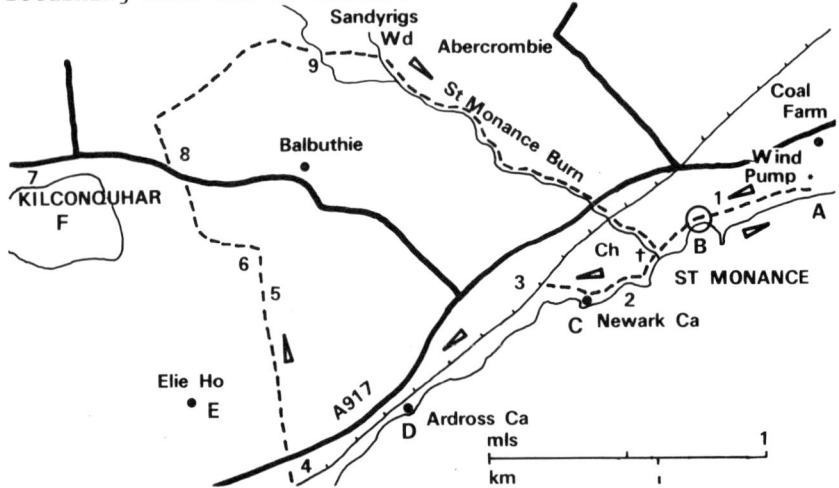

1 GR 525 016. From St Monance harbour climb street to the east and walk along cliff top to the round tower (saltpans windpump) and return.
2 Round shore roads and across burn to the church. Cliff path to Newark Castle and down steps to the shore.
3 Faster progress can be made along the old railway track but leave to look at Ardross Castle and scramble down to shore to view the coal seam (in the cliff below).
4 Continue along railway till a stone dyke projects onto the shore. Two gates line up inland leading to A917. Walk left as far as corner of wall round wood, 'Elie Estate', and turn up farm track.
5 At end of track go straight on to gate into wood. Turn right and cross ditch, left then back again.
6 Keep pond on your right and go up grassy track to road.
7 A diversion here is suggested through the well kept village to the red sandstone church and round the new cemetery by a path to a viewing point for bird watchers.
8 Return to the strip of woodland to the north of the St Monance road you had passed earlier and walk up track to road round the Kilconquhar Castle Estate. Turn right.
9 After end of wood on your left, follow fence round to the right past the sharp bend in the burn till you come to rails at a cattle drinking place where you can cross the burn. Head for wicket gate against wood and cross through ride to far field. Follow burn down to shore.

A A rectangular basin can be seen at low tide from which sea water was led in via a cut channel to a pipe and was pumped up into the iron pans heated by low grade coal. One building has been partially excavated but is subject to constant erosion by wave action.
B St Monance is an active ship building and repairing harbour and the west slipway is seldom empty.
C Newark Castle appears to have been occupied in 1645.
D Ardross Castle was built in 1370; the headland is now badly eroded by the sea The coal seam can be reached over tumbled blocks. Sandstone layers show marked sea bottom ripples.
E Elie House, latterly a convent, is now a health farm, but the forestry is independently managed.
F Kilconquhar Loch, once presumed to be the result of blocked drainage. A recent survey suggests that excavation for peat is at least partly responsible.

A well managed estate with large specimen trees, an attractive burn and traditional parkland. Fine views from Balcarres Craig and Kilbrackmont.

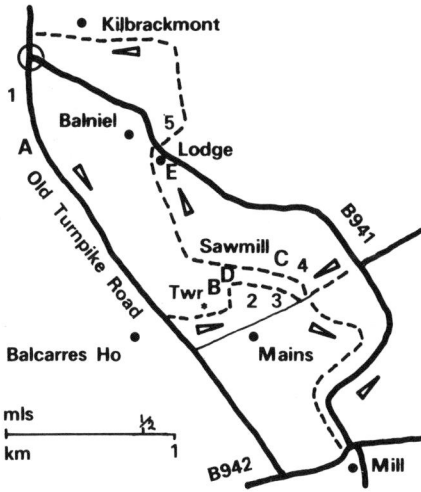

1 GR 468 060. Walk south along old road. After white gate and entering woods turn left and climb narrow track to left of quarry. Descend ridge beyond tower and curve left along narrow belt of trees. Turn sharp right.

2 Parts of the path at the edge of the den have fallen away, but try to return to the fence path.

3 The zig-zag path through thick shrubs may be difficult to find (gap by boulder with beech beyond). Keep cottages on your right.

4 On returning keep to the right of the burn and sawmill.

5 Through field gate across to corner of wood and turn left past triangular copse. Follow field boundary up to double walled farm track. Turn left.

A You are on the old Cupar to Elie road, turnpiked in 1810, and a milestone can be seen at 468 056, sadly minus its cast iron cap. The diversion to the line of the present main road after 1828, not only removed traffic from the vicinity of the house but also avoided the steep hill.

B The romantic structure is placed at a viewpoint covering the whole of the Forth valley and eastern Fife.

C As in many such woodlands rhododendrons have taken up much of the floor, but their flowers can be spectacular as early as April. Fine mature larch and beech have grown in the shelter of the den, and the owner has planted many young trees. Plastic sleeves protect against deer and accelerate growth but make cosy homes for hungry voles.

D Although the sawmill is no longer powered by water, the mill dam has recently been renovated, with a refuge for waterfowl in the centre.

E The lodge, with its small figure on the roof and the splendid gateway with heraldic beasts on the pillars were designed by Sir Robert Lorimer of Kellie Castle.

21

Up on the broad East Neuk ridge, we start off along a hard road serving several farms, make our way to a disused railway and down the south slope with views of the Forth and the fishing ports. A winding track takes us to the north end of Balcarres Den and back through the former mining village of Largo Ward.

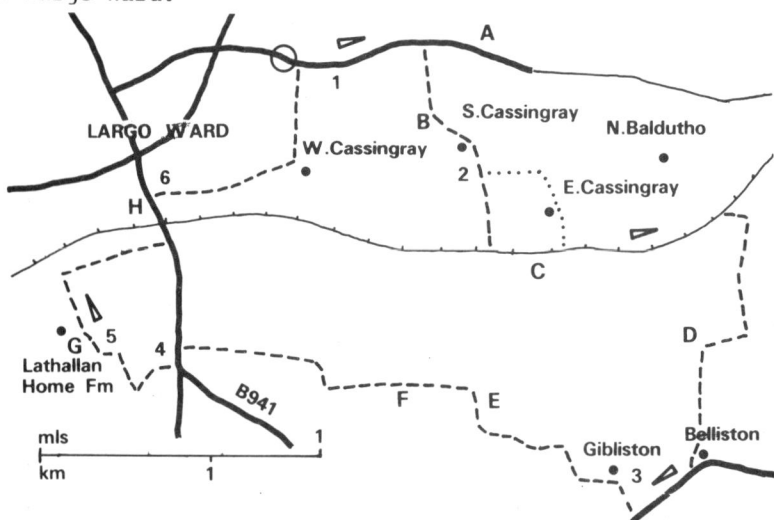

1 GR 471 079. Head east along metalled road to the sign to South Cassingray. At farmstead, through to left and past wide metal gate between buildings.
2 At field, over wooden rails by gate and, if crops permit, south along far side of fence to the railway cutting. Otherwise, turn left along raised grassy track and round the field to East Cassingray and through to the old railway.
3 Past the cottages, turn right to Gibliston farm, continue along walled track, skirting a wood on your left.
4 An interesting loop can be taken by turning left to reach the north end of the old turnpike road through Balcarres and then turning right past a lodge between rhododendrons.
5 Follow farm road past walled garden and turn right. Turn right again at T junction and you are soon back on the B941.
6 Turn right to Balcarres Ward and continue to corner cottage at West Cassingray. A track across the fields to the north brings you back onto the road along which you started.

A Some of the land is still poorly drained and in winter often carries large flocks of wild geese.
B The cottages are of irregular blocks of dark dolerite, with quoins of squared sandstone. The pantile roof is typically Fife and the double windows were often an indication of domestic weaving.
C The railway was meant to connect Leven with St Andrews by an inland route, but was only built as far as Lochty GR 522 080., where a short section is still maintained as a private railway and may be visited in summer.
D the quarry was worked for roadstone until recently and large blocks of dolerite lie near the entrance.
E The zigzag track dates from before 1775.
F A mixed cover of light woodland and clearings provides a habitat favoured by chaffinches and titmice.
G The walled garden has a gazebo with Venetian style windows, blocked in on one side.
H Note the disused colliery shafts in the fields, left. Many of the cottages in the village were built for miners and coal was being transported from here by rail up to 1913.

This gaunt and isolated tower house stands by a ridge road from Kingsbarns to Largo Ward, and a circular walk explores old tracks between farms and returns past a preserved remnant of an inland railway.

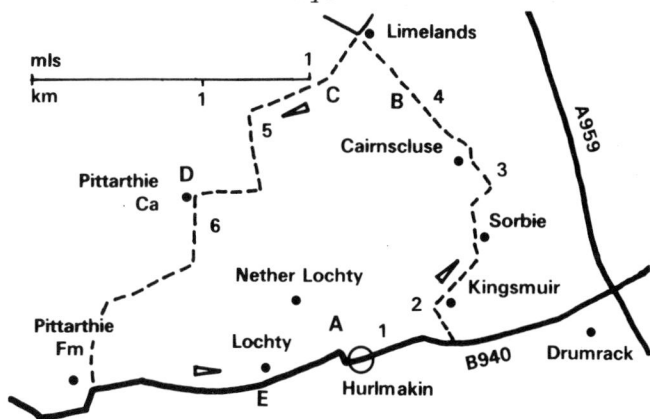

1 GR 530 082. Walk along road to past end of belt of woodland on right and turn left past Kingsmuir House front.
2 Leave the farm buildings on your right and after a bend head for Sorbie, a stone building with asbestos roof and a ruined cottage. Go round to the left and head for an isolated cottage and Cairnscluse farmstead beyond.
3 Row of cottages ahead; route really goes just to the right, but go round the garden and pick up the strip of rough grass and ditch at the side of the field beyond. Keep going and you are into the track proper, between two hedges.
4 After crossing a burn by a pond continue to cross roads by cottage and turn left onto concrete road to Chesters Farm. Through farmstead and up grassy track ahead.
5 Opposite a gap in the wall, right, turn left and pass a gate with conifer plantation beyond which you skirt on your left. At farm buildings in far corner turn right up to the tower house.
6 Take farm track down slope to south, which switches to right of wall. On reaching ditch turn right and follow track round past Pittarthie Farm and onto road. Turn left and down road to start.

A The short part of the zigzag is part of a road from Pittenweem to St Andrews, used in the early 18th century. Pittarthie Castle can be seen from the grassed over section to the north which went close to it.
B This is also one of the many routes from St Andrews to the south coast, crossing the burns upstream of the difficult dens, such as the Kenly Burn near Boarhills (Walk 31).
C We ascend the first part of the ridge road with views towards St Andrews. A long strip of woodland east of Kinaldy marks the line of the old Pittenweem road.
D A plaque over a window reads 1653. By this date there was a greater feeling of security, and residences were becoming less defensive in design (compare Scotstarvit, Walk 25). There were still gun ports near ground level and iron grills over certain windows.
E The Lochty railway from Kennoway has been preserved by the owner of Lochty Farm and rolling stock from many sources can be identified. It is open to the public in the summer. The line was originally intended to continue to St Andrews.

Walk 22   ROUND KIPPO AND AIRFIELD   8.5 miles (13.6 km)

This section of the disused track between St Andrews and Crail is a reservoir for wild life and leads to one of the forgotten airfields of the Second World War. Woodland and farm tracks lead through typical East Neuk landscape to the southern end of the railway.

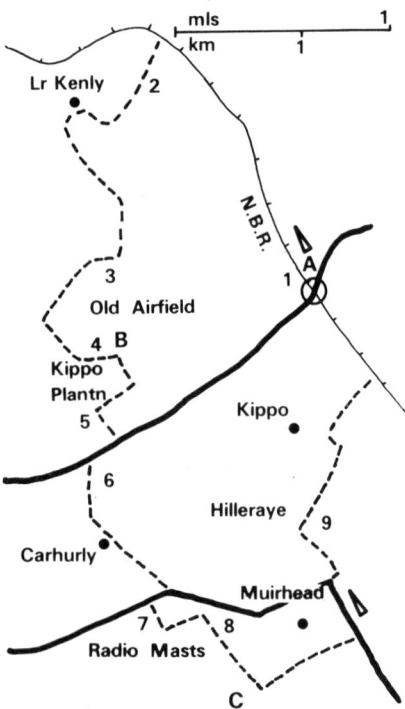

1 GR 580 114. Cross platform and descend to grassy track. At Boarhills turn down left before small bridge.

2 Along farm road and down to Lower Kenly steading. A diversion to the bridge north of the farm house is well worth the trouble. Then carry on south past the cottages to Upper Kenly.

3 Pass round the south (left) side of the nearest hangar and continue round the perimeter track past last concrete hut.

4 After series of small brick buildings on your right, head for left corner of wood. Through a wicket gate beyond the burn and along the edge of the field till a second wicket gate. Turn right and follow rabbit fence round plantation.

5 Keep plantation in view until corner of a deer fence seen, cross a deep ditch and follow tractor wheel track to road. Turn right.

6 Turn left along grass strip to gate through Carhurly farm.

7 Turn left through woodland towards building with radio masts. At the entrance turn left along grass strip with wheel tracks. Turn right beyond north end of belt of trees and along edge of field.

8 Walk along road in woodland strip. Turn left at main road. At corner turn right to pass Hilleraye.

9 The route continues right, along a tractor track across a field. At the cottages by the burn, turn right along field edge and left at the old railway back to start.

A The stationmaster´s garden included tree lupins, privet, apples.

B Good stream section with a thin coal seam to right of wicket gate.

C A diversion to the southwest gives a glimpse of Airdrie House with its 16th century tower and its fine avenue towards the Forth. Part of a route to Carnbee and Kellie.

From the fringes of the port we pass through the Kilminning nature reserve to Fife Ness where migrating birds are often seen and a coastguard station controls the whole east coast. Fine views across to Grampians and islands of the Forth.

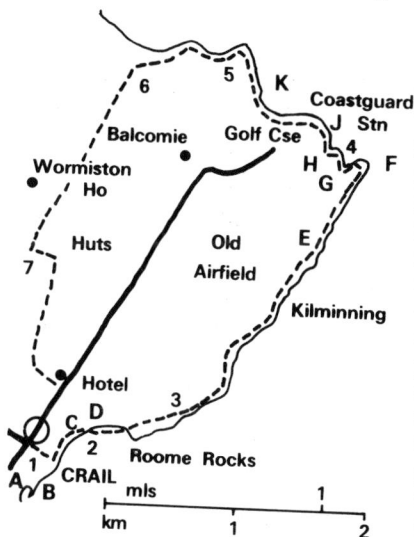

1 GR 613 077. Take the Tolbooth Wynd to Nethergate; turn right then left past white cottage by the side of the burn, turn left.
2 Follow lower path and, if tide permits, cross the shore to the red sandstone cliffs. Clamber up by the cobble slipway.
3 After road through caravans follow the well used track to the coastguard station.
4 Rounding the lighthouse you join the access road but turn along white posts, right, at the fairway.
5 At end of golf course, you pass through a gate in a field wall and continue inside field to next gate. Turn left.
6 Head up hollow to gate and continue past farmstead.
7 At end of belt of trees behind wall, turn left and then right at corner of airfield buildings. Follow fence to caravans, turn left to road by hotel and right to start.

A Trail guide to buildings from the post office.
B The burn is the tail race from a mill at Rumford, near the National Trust houses (trail guide p.11).
C Across the water the Isle of May with its white lighthouse is a bird reserve and can be visited by boat from Anstruther
D The cylindrical dovecot, c. 16th century, belonged to Crail Priory and was latterly painted white as a seamark. To landward note the struggle of plot owners to shield gardens.
E Beyond the headland dense thickets of blackthorn fill the hollows and as you climb the cliff before the coastguard houses an arched bush on your left shows clearly the wind's inhibiting effect.
F Past the light a low platform is exposed except at high tides and contains large deep pools full of marine life.
G The caravans, with their lawns and rock gardens, stand where there was a small fishing village, of which only one cottage remains. Sea stack nearby was site of a lime kiln.
H You pass a small platform in the rock with a circular channel centred on a shallow hole.
J A curious iron 'sentry box', half buried in the turf, is believed to have been a form of sea mine. The lifeboat house, made redundant by the helicopter, now stores groundsman's tools and the slipway is a tee. Marram grass beyond remains as reminder of pre golf course terrain.
K Lying amongst sand and seaweed is an erratic block of dolerite, known as the blue stone, possibly dropped by floating ice.

One of the easterly routes across Fife has always come this
way and the old tower house of Scotstarvit stands by it. The
connection between the laird´s home farm and the mill was
also valuable and now takes us down to the banks of the
River Eden. Crawford Priory grounds are seen, as well as the
parish church and lime hills of Cults. An awkward river bank
path in places, otherwise easy.

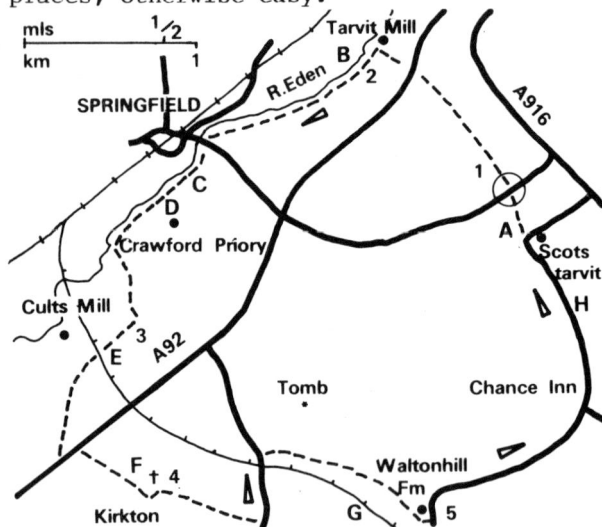

1 GR 369 116. A car may be parked by the entrance to
Scotstarvit on the A916 as in Walk 25. Go down double walled
green road and across main road past caravan site.
2 Tracks along the river bank are mostly for anglers and
require some agility in places. After going under the road
bridge, carry on along the bank past a footbridge, turning
left opposite the next mill, along the woodland edge.
3 Join the drive to Crawford Priory and bear right to a
cross roads where you carry straight on, leaving the farm
buildings on your right; then by a lodge to reach the A92.
4 After the church turn left round garden of the manse, then
bear right past cottage and along edge of field to road.
Turn left. After crossing burn, take farm track to the right
and bear right along first fence line up across the hill
through Walton Hill farmstead to the road. Turn left.
5 Follow the road to Chance Inn. At the T junction straight
on through the rest of the village and past Scotstarvit.

A Scotstarvit lies on an old route across Fife and an Act
allowed it to be diverted round the house in 1629. The old
road to Cupar curves round along the field (and parish)
boundary from this point; our route downhill is an original
road and at least as old.
B Little remains of the mill but two walls and a bridge over
the outflow channel.
C Note the reed filled curling pond on your left.
D Here you can see the remains of Crawford Priory with its
elegant Gothic chapel.
E The road is crossed here by the track of a railway
connection from Cults Lime Works to the main line and the
ruin of a bridge across the Eden may also be found.
F Church built in 1793 when the Rev David Wilkie, the father
of David Wilkie the painter, was minister.
G Note embankment, the mineral railway from Cults limeworks.
H Much of the metalling of the old road appears to be
undisturbed; little public money would have been spent on it
after 1800, when the turnpike, now the A916, took its place.

Walk 25 HILL OF TARVIT AND MUIRHEAD   6 miles (9.6 km)

A visit to the beautifully kept house and its fine garden can be combined with a walk taking us to a viewpoint by the house and then by Scotstarvit Tower and along two historic ways from Cupar and Ceres to the south.

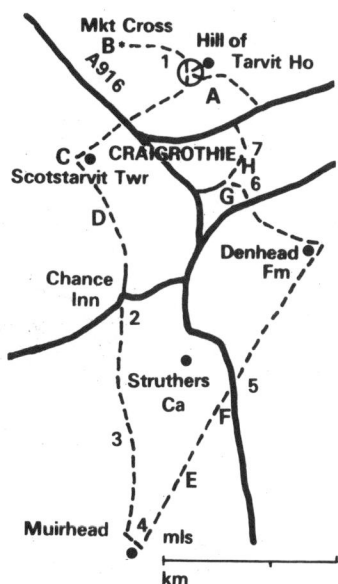

1 GR 379 119. A car can be parked at Hill of Tarvit to climb the hill. You can then go along the west drive to Scotstarvit. Turn left past the farm, over the brae to Chance Inn.

2 After modern road turns right, turn left on gravel drive past last cottage, Restalrig. At next cottages go between them and through wicket gate into field. Go round field to the left and keep against wall until next corner when you climb over to the other side.

3 Back again after crossing burn on single stone footbridge. Continue up grass strip to road by cottage and turn left.

4 Past last cottage garden on left and through at corner. Follow wall on left, either side. Mind young trees at end.

5 Continue to Denhead Farm and turn left before the house.

6 Cross lower main road and on down narrow track between walls. Turn up left past a dovecot and on to a T junction. Turn right.

7 Over packhorse bridge and on reaching road at top, turn right and back to start via east drive.

A House, formerly Wemyss Hall, redesigned by Lorimer in 1904. Furnished interior open to public (National Trust). Across walled garden up to fine iron gates, then a path to a direction guide at the summit.

B Good view here over the Howe with Crawford Priory below. On your right you can trace the old road from Kennoway to Cupar.

C Scotstarvit Tower was a typical small laird's house of the early 17th century.

D The old road is here still in good condition having been maintained as a highway up to 1800, when it was replaced by the A916, left.

E You are now on the Bishop's Road, so named after Archbishop Sharp of St Andrews who was murdered on the road in 1679.

F Just beyond the ruins of Struthers Castle, Scotstarvit lines up with the Hope monument, and Norman's Law is seen to the right.

G Ruined lectern type doocot on left; fancy fowls may be seen after the junction.

H Marriage lintel right '17 WM MP 50

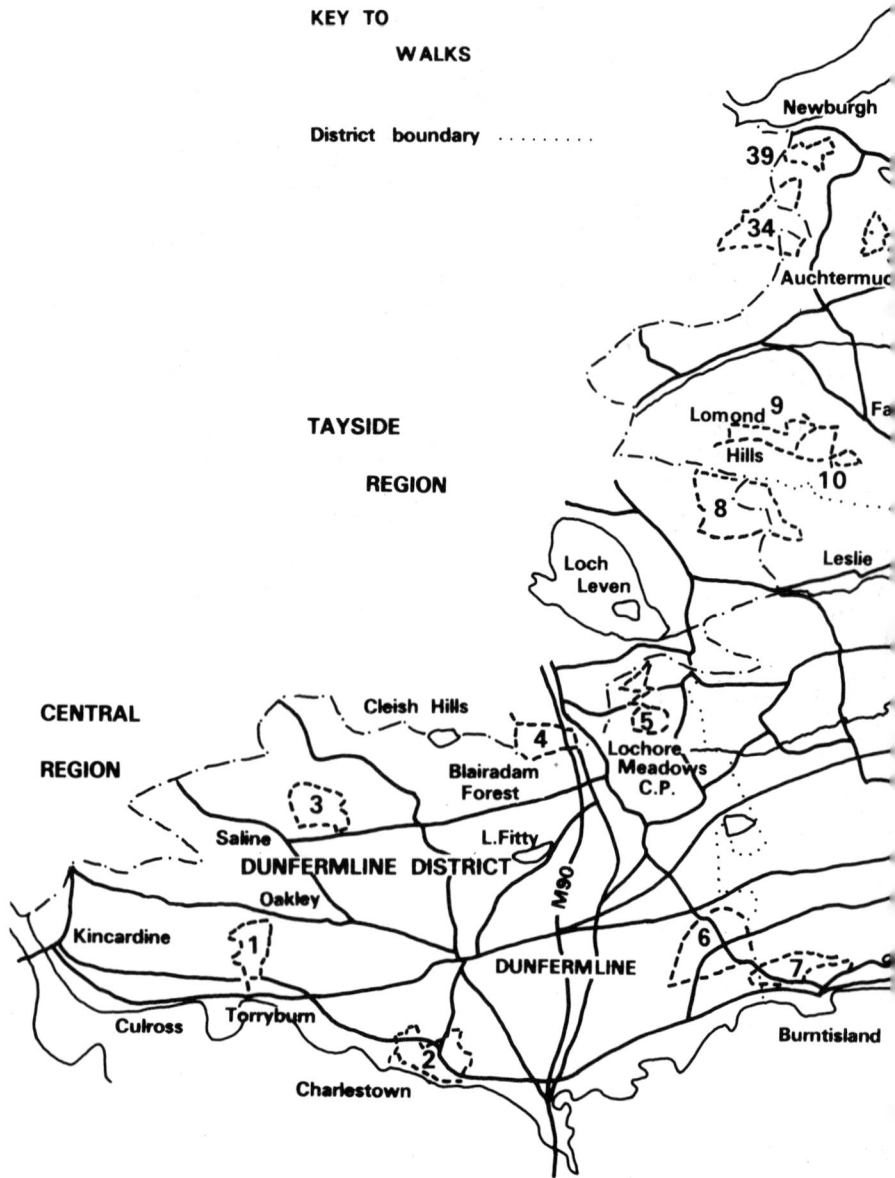

KEY TO

WALKS

District boundary ·········

TAYSIDE

REGION

CENTRAL

REGION

Newburgh

39

34

Auchtermu

Lomond 9   Fa
Hills
8   10

Loch
Leven

Leslie

Cleish Hills

4

5

Lochore
Meadows
C.P.

Blairadam
Forest

3

Saline

L.Fitty

DUNFERMLINE DISTRICT

Oakley

M90

Kincardine

1

6

DUNFERMLINE

7

Culross   Torryburn

2

Burntisland

Charlestown

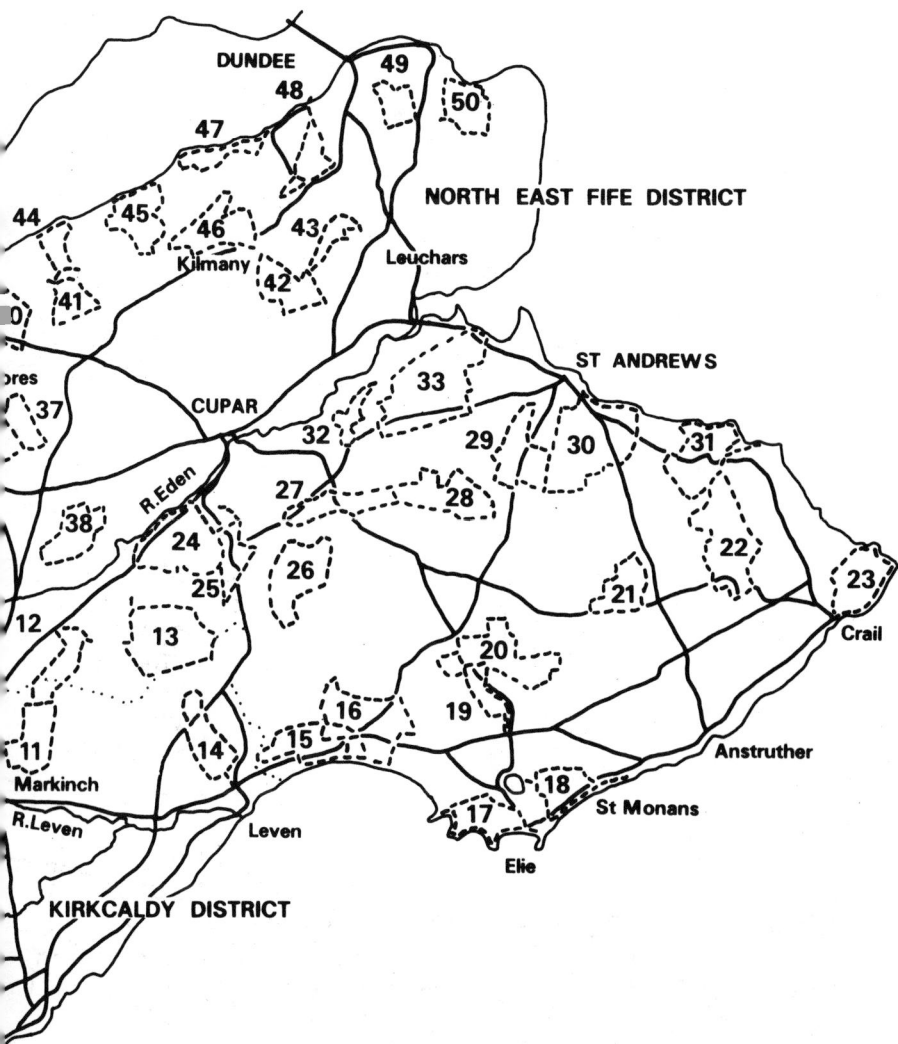

DUNDEE

48

49

47

50

44 45

46 43

NORTH EAST FIFE DISTRICT

Kilmany 42

Leuchars

0 41

res

37

CUPAR

33

ST ANDREWS

32

29

30

31

R.Eden

27

28

38

24

22

26

25

23

21

Crail

12

13

20

11

14

15

16

19

Markinch

18

Anstruther

R.Leven

17

St Monans

Leven

Elie

KIRKCALDY DISTRICT

RKCALDY

29

We start by a burn in a wooded den, a local nature reserve, and climb up to the surrounding countryside. With alternating field and woodland, the walk has its rough sections and steep scrambles. Nature trail guide from P.O.

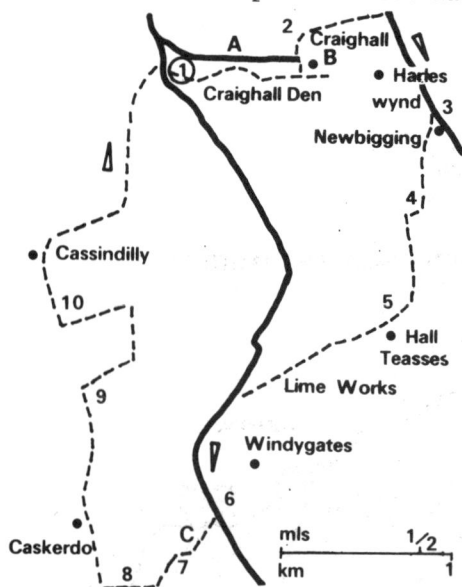

1 GR 399 108. A car may be parked at the entrance to Craighall Den. At Craighall Farm, limekiln on your right and quarry with caves on your left. Return to farm and leave steading on your right. Turn left along farm track as far as cottage and by gate to the right.

2 Continue along edge of field to road. Right to Newbigging.

3 At the nearest building turn right and pass round rear to old bridge over the burn. Continue up upper edge of field.

4 At the top by a ruined cottage turn right along wall to corner of plantation and then left along hedge line to farm track. Turn right

5 Past Hall Teasses steading and follow farm track past iron gate entrance to Teasses Lime Works. Continue to road and turn left.

6 Follow road until it enters a second wood, past Windygates entrance. Just before a cottage on the right, Korrigan, turn right past a bar to a soft wheel track into the wood.

7 Where the track opens out into a wider clearing look for a wheel track half left downhill. There is a deep trench to the left and the track follows an irregular ridge down to a wicket gate.

8 Up line of trees to farm track in strip of woodland. Turn right and follow past Carskerdo Farm.

9 Track continues along upper edge of two fields, then turns downhill. Follow upper side of next fence on the level and turn up left at far end onto your original line.

10 Continue past Cassindilly Farm on good farm track down to the road.

A Old quarry, left, in dolerite. Note weathering into rounded blocks and penetration by tree roots.

B There was an important house on this site by which ran a main road into Ceres, part of which remains north of the cottage.

C Coal was worked near Teasses Den in the last century and limestone was burnt in clamps in shallow troughs in the ground which may still be seen.

Two typical East Neuk east-west ridges take us in the direction of the east coast. Both were used for carrying coal and are now left to the walker and the occasional farm vehicle. On the return a view of the Ceres valley and the hills beyond is a reward for a gentle climb.

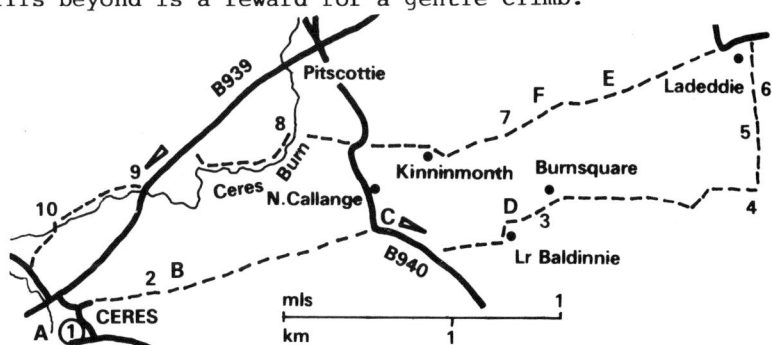

1 GR 401 114. Cars may be parked across the burn from the Folk Museum. Walk over the cobbled packhorse bridge and turn right. Turn left at the Anstruther road and then right up School Hill. Enter field at the end and follow edge to stile
2 Continue up the bank and through a wood. Beyond this through a gateway in a field to the next wood where there is a stile at the corner. Grass path, farm track to the B940.
3 After passing farm buildings, left, you see a white gate ahead. The entrance drive to Burnsquare curves round to the left but you go straight on past a pond along a grassy wheel track. Through a dilapidated gate to a ford with stepping stones downstream. Over gate to grass track flanked by trees
4 Where avenue ends, pass through a gateway between cross walls and take a gateway, left. Then down slope to the burn.
5 Footbridge collapsed. Use stepping stones a little below the fence and go up the grassy strip by wall.
6 Switch to right side of wall as far as the road and turn left. Continue straight on along ridge at corner.
7 Between two rows of ancient hawthorns to a road winding down to Kinninmonth Farm. At main road turn left across bridge then right along track below cottages.
8 Cross old stone bridge and then turn left along far bank, keeping to the ridge. Where a footbridge appears on the left, turn right to reach gate onto main road. Turn left.
9 At entrance to Ceres Mill, over rails beside bridge and along edge of field north of the burn.
10 At installation, pass between metal fence and burn and cross bridge. Right of Meldrum Hotel and across green.

A The bridge here was recorded in the 17th century, and in 1786 it was deemed unsuitable as 'a Bridge for Wheel Carriages but only for passengers on foot and Horseback'. Farm implements in the folk museum can be seen on your left.
B The disturbed ground in the wood marks the site of coal workings, supplying Ceres and Cupar.
C The plaque to Lunardi was placed there at the bicentenary
D Just past the Z bend at Baldinnie the road surface shows spheroidal weathering typical of dolerite. At other levels coal and limestone bands were easily accessible from valley sides and pits were worked within the last hundred years.
E We are on another coal road, built by Cupar and St Andrews in the 1780s, with branch to limestone quarries on the north This is typical of a late 18th century statute labour road.
F Ceres lies at the head of a flat valley, probably a glacial lake floor, and Hill of Tarvit lies beyond, with its column, to the right of West Lomond hill. Note the old road through Callange over the abandoned bridge to Cupar.

A wild upland scene near to St Andrews. Continues the two ridges of Walk 27 eastwards and shows features of geological interest. Given patience to wait or move quietly a variety of waterfowl on the reservoir may be seen.

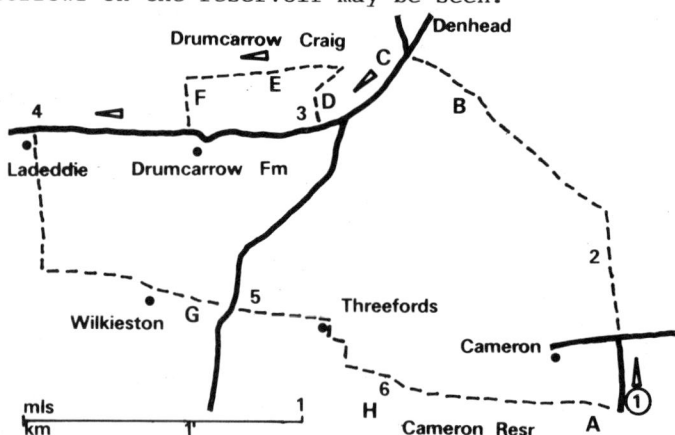

1 GR 479 114. Though the space is primarily for anglers, a car may be parked by the end of the dam. Return to the approach road to the farm and cross to a track along the edge of the wood.

2 A rough strip of gorse is prickly but negotiable, and leads to a pleasant wheel track all the way to the Denhead crossroads through a belt of woodland.

3 A track leads past a quarry round to the right and then turns back along the ridge. A rough wooden barrier at the far corner of the enclosure leads to a farm track down to the left, past cottages and towards Drumcarrow farm.

4 At Ladeddie Farm turn left down the farm track. This ceases after the first field and at the next opening you will need to switch to leave the wall on your left. Cross burn by stepping stones and climb up along field edge to the southern ridge road and turn left.

5 Cross the public road and carry straight on along raised grassy strip past the ruined buildings and turn right. Turn left this side of the ditch and along to the second corner.

6 Here you can either cross the swampy ditch by the wooden rails and reach the end of the reservoir dam (grassy bank ahead), or go round the conifer plantation, along the line of electricity poles and down a wall to the path along the north shore of the reservoir back to the start. Another option is to cross the dam and there is an attractive path on the south side.

A The reservoir supplies St Andrews and attracts many species of waterfowl. Boats for fishing may be hired at the water bailiff's house.

B Limestone was quarried where left half of the wood grows.

C Ironstone workings can be seen to the west of the cottage.

D Remains of an iron age broch lie to your left and in face of quarry ahead the dolerite rock shows columnar jointing.

E A fine view of the Eden estuary and Strathkinness village from the ridge. Below you is the Denork reservoir and house. This side of Strathkinness a strip of woodland on a low ridge marks the line of the Bishop's Road (see Walk 33).

F Viewed end on, the jointing forms a polygonal pattern.

G South of Wilkieston Farm, old limestone quarries are overgrown with scrub and are in the same strata as those at Backfield of Ladeddie on the south side of the ridge.

H Bad drainage in this shallow valley is now aggravated by the barrier of the reservoir dam and explains the extensive area of rushes.

32

From the outskirts of St Andrews we follow part of the old railway track as it winds its way between the ridges to the south. Farm roads lead us round to the A915, from which we go cross country to descend Lumbo Den.

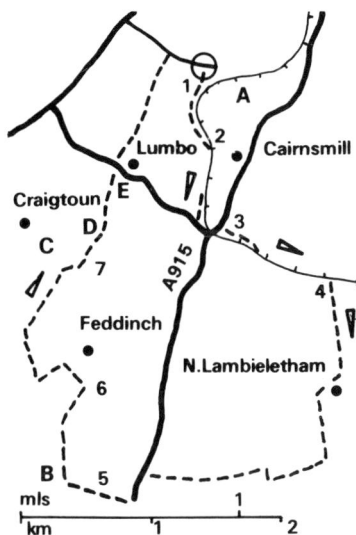

1 GR 494 155. Park in a side road off the Canongate just beyond the junction with John Knox Road. An open space leads to the Cairnsmill Burn which we keep to our left up the den.

2 Beyond where the railway embankment crosses the burn a gentle slope leads up to the track, which may be followed as far as a pile of earth and stones. This must be scrambled up to a patch of rough ground against a fence, left. Follow the fence to meet the road ahead to the right of the old railway bridge and turn left to the A915.

3 Cross to the entrance road to Wester Balrymonth, but turn right past the railings and walk along the side of the burn.

4 Turn right at the isolated cottage and follow the farm track to the second farmstead, South Lambieletham. Turn right through Priorletham and left at the A915.

5 A farm track between walls leads to the right past a ruined cottage into a scrub fringed tunnel. When you reach the wood proper, at the corner of the rushy field, turn right between the woodland edge and the field. At the next corner you will see round to the left a grassy strip which you follow down to a burn. A farm track goes to Feddinch.

6 Turn left up the slope and left again at the top along a grassy track. Turn right at next field boundary and follow down to the wood. Bear right along edge of field and cross the burn. Right along road to bowling green and turn right.

7 Follow the path down the den and, where it crosses the lowest footbridge to turn back, continue down the western edge of the den to the road at Lumbo Bridge. A gate opposite leads to Lumbo Den and a stile at the far end leads to a gravel path back to the Canongate. Turn right to start.

A The railway curved round the south side of John Knox Road (now through back gardens) and then south along the burn. It was closed in 1969 and many an airman must have taken the train to Kingsbarns or a Fleet Air Arm pilot to Crail.

B 'Waterless' may seem a misnomer for this wood, but it may be derived from 'water leas', which is a fair description of the field on your right.

C Craigtoun estate was bought by the Younger family, of brewing fame and the house, of red sandstone, was built in 1903. It is now a home for the elderly and its grounds are a fun park as you can see.

D Footpaths in den have been recently restored and planted.

E The Canongate, from which we started, came through Denhead and Craigtoun and can be traced to right of the wood ahead.

Across the open landscape south of St Andrews and round to
the coast between the Rock and Spindle and East Sands. An
easy walk, mostly along well-defined tracks with good views
across Tentsmuir and to the Angus coast.

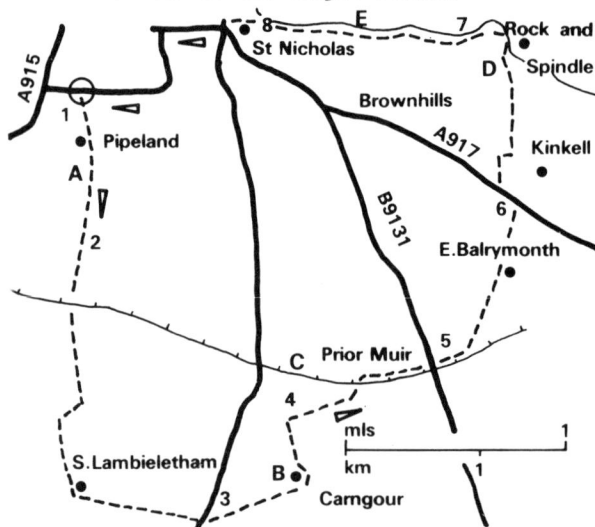

1 GR 506 154. A car can be left in Scooniehill Road, the
last turning to the left along the Largo road (A915).
Pipeland Walk is a path into town, and the path opposite
leads up past Pipeland Farm passing the water works on your
left.
2 At farm road go downhill across old railway by cottage and
up past the steadings of N. and S. Lambieletham. Turn left.
3 Continue past gate along raised grass strip which you
follow round to Carngour. Past the house and turn left
beyond buildings.
4 Turn right along grassy track. Over bridge to B9131.
5 Straight past the old railway station and turn left down
farm track at line of Scots pine. At Easter Balrymonth farm
go right then left through the steading and down to the main
road.
6 Go left to first wall on north side and along it to farm
road. Turn right, then left at T junction, down to shore.
7 Round to the left on the grass between the cliffs and the
shore till a footbridge and a small gate with steps up to
the top path. Follow to East Sands past the caravan site.
8 Past the new swimming pool building and turn left. Return
to start along Lamond Drive, turning left into Kilrymont
Road, leading to Scooniehill Road.

A Above the waterworks look back across St Andrews to the
famous golf course, Tentsmuir Forest and Dundee.
B Decorative barge boards in the gable end of the farmhouse.
C Hardly a trace remains of the ballast of the old track.
D A mass of hardened volcanic debris surrounds the upright
Rock and the Spindle, with its radiating columns of basalt.
Inclined folds in the sedimentary strata form an arresting
pattern along this coast, especially at low tide.
E The Maiden Rock is a fossil sea stack left stranded by the
post-glacial rise of the land. Both the upper and lower
cliff levels are good examples of raised beaches on one of
which most of St Andrews stands, while the caravans are
split between two beaches.

Walk 31   KENLY BURN AND KITTOCK´S DEN   6.5 miles (10.5 km)
Combines a stretch of coast of geological interest with two
unspoilt dens, in the larger of which there is evidence for
several water mills. We can see the importance of the creeks
and bays related to the folded strata as places to collect
seaweed and launch small boats. The grotesque Buddo Rock
stands well above the present shore, but at low tide we can
clamber over the tidal zone.

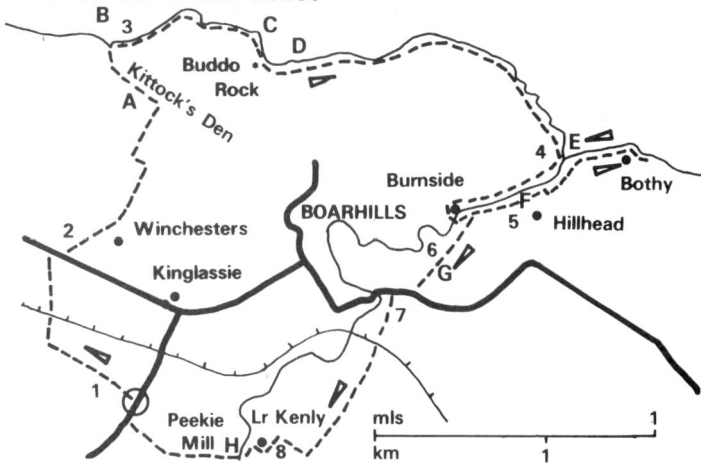

1 GR 554 130. Take double dyked track and at the wood turn
right to follow left of fence to main road past deserted
cottages.
2 Down tree bordered entrance to Winchesters Farm, cross
grass right of cottage. Follow zig-zag track to den and sea.
3 Follow coastal path to right. The raised beach is soggy
from seepage from the base of the fossil cliff but there are
stepping stones in the worst places.
4 Only the agile can cross directly to reach bothy, others
follow field edge up the den, turn left past Burnside
farmhouse down to a footbridge. Turn L and follow dry mill
lade to disused mill near Hillhead Farm. Climb bank and turn
left after gap in wall by farm, down farm track to shore.
Walk past fishermen´s bothy to old harbour.
5 Return by same route up to the gap in the wall by Hillhead
Farm, down to disused mill and walk up dry mill lade. At
footbridge climb up left to second mill.
6 Pass miller´s house, dry millpond and to left of cottages.
7 Turn left up grass track and continue SW past Lower Kenly
Farm. The view from the road bridge is recommended.
8 Turn right before steading buildings by round horse engine
house with wind vane. Follow track upstream to Peekie Bridge
Take vehicle road past miller´s house to near start.

A Tread quietly and you may see deer. The yellow irises in
the damp bottom, the bluebells and red campion are
spectacular in season.
B Many of the beach pebbles of deep red shelly limestone,
have iron ore in bands, or are rhythmically patterned.
C Seaward of the Buddo Rock a dark brown sandstone layer
lies on an almost white band. As the latter has been
attacked by the waves the great blocks above have tumbled.
D Note the several seaweed roads down to the beach.
E More contorted strata as you approach the bothy. In the
harbour beyond, inclined bedding planes show numerous
impressions of the stems and branches of coal forest trees.
F Note the date on the gable of the old mill. The mill lade
came from a dam just below Burnside farm cottages.
G The miller´s house has the date 1790 on the NE skewput.
H The coping stones of the parapets are cleverly interlocked
and the arms of Prior Hepburn (c.1500) are on the south face.

A varied and beautiful area of woodland with excellent views from a commanding position overlooking the Eden estuary and the Howe of Fife. Many old sandstone quarries overgrown with ferns and mosses.

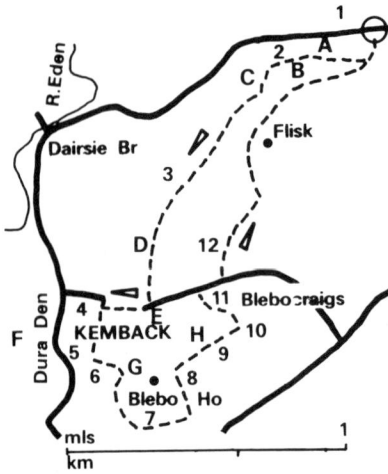

1 GR 435 165. If car spaces are occupied there is a layby down the road. Up the grassy track, turn right at gate. Along lower edge of wood till end of conifer plantations, then turn up the slope

2 A stand of Scots pine, right, fringed with birch, then you meet a downhill loop of a tractor track. Turn right, uphill.

3 At fork go right and reach to edge of wood and past houses. Right at the road and down the steps to Kemback.

4 Leave church on your left. At seat above steps on left climb over bank and join woodland path to left.

5 Turn right past cottage overlooking side den. Over little stone bridge and past ends of wood rails. Round wood to left

6 Skirt round left side of hillock and continue to corner.

7 Take metal gate on right into field and follow edge to the left. A metal wicket gate takes you on to drive. Turn left.

8 Past walled garden and straight on up grassy track ahead. At corner turn right by telephone pole into wood.

9 Where field ends on the right, curve uphill to narrow opening by yew and through wooden wicket gate right to path along edge.

10 At road turn left and then right at T junction. After Viewfield turn left. Pass Thornbank (farmstead) up on your right and after two fields turn right past Craig Hill. Right at large pine tree.

11 Carry on past Post Office and left at conifer plantation.

12 Road curves round to right but take narrow path through woodrush, left. You come to a wheel track between two plantations which turns right along a third fence. At far end keep right over uneven ground and across a dip to a deep track in woodrush. This meets an old track which winds downhill. One young plantation may be crossed between two stiles; continue on the old track to the first gate.

A Across Eden valley you can see the pink Lucklaw quarry.

B On your left a stand of western hemlock.

C Small areas are being planted using plastic tubes and stakes, while larger areas are fenced against rabbits. The growth of a young tree is said to be twice as fast in tubes.

D A Marvellous view here across to the Lomonds, Trossachs.

E Curious pairing of beech with oak, with decorative roots.

F Dura Den is worth a separate visit, but you can glimpse a water powered mill and weavers´ cottages along the road.

G Near the boathouse the red of the dogwood and the yellow of the willows make a pleasing contrast in winter.

H Blebo Craigs, a scattered village has been much added to in our century, but originated as a settlement for quarrymen and weavers. On your right the Bishop´s Road runs along the next ridge towards St Andrews. Archbishop Sharp was murdered in 1679 a little further along, at Magus Muir.

The scene of the murder of Archbishop Sharp in 1679 on Magus Muir is a reminder of both the religious struggle and the nature of highways at the time. The walk also passes large modern farmsteads, fossil cliffs, a salt-marsh nature reserve and the quarries from which much of St Andrews was built.

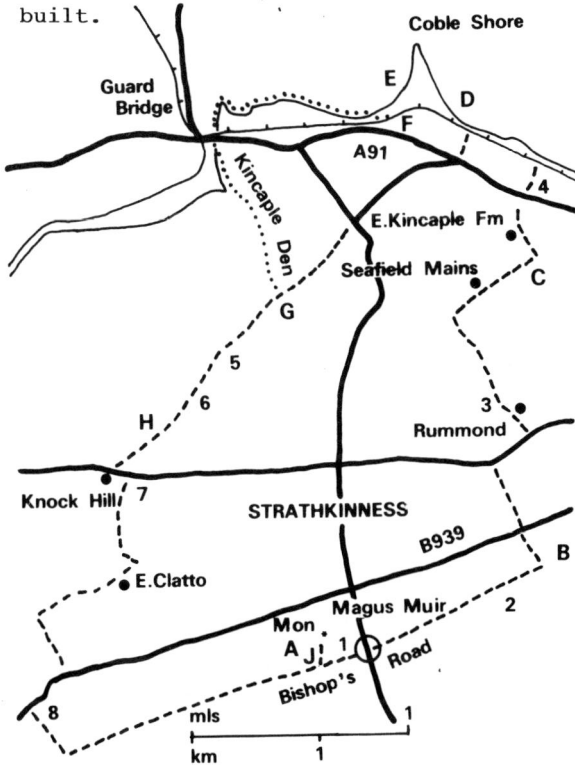

1 GR 459 152. To the monument and return. Take track opposite to the east and follow the strip of trees.
2 Continue along same line at end of trees unless crops may be damaged, when alternative route should be used.
3 Through white gate and paddock beyond cottage. Left of fence and wall down to Seafield Mains.
4 Keep right of fence to reach shore path along old railway.
5 After passing strip of woodland, head for farm on skyline.
6 North of new bungalow: head to right of trees round quarry. Pass through long field between scrub woodland to reach road.
7 Through metal gate up grass strip. Round new garden.
8 Through metal gate and up cart track to corner of wood. Left through wood and then follow fence line along ridge.

A The murder is depicted in Holy Trinity Church, St Andrews.
B The road crossed the Claremont Burn near Dewar´s Mill.
C The steep slopes here facing the estuary are the remains of cliffs along successive post-glacial shorelines.
D Alluvium and blown sand have built out the present shore; extensive tidal mud attract large numbers of wading birds.
E A former crossing place to Coble Point opposite. A low tide diversion to the Guard Bridge is shown. Best to scramble up between the two road bridges to avoid mud.
F The toll house was erected before 1818 at the minimum distance a second toll could be charged from Cupar East toll bar (six miles, as milestone indicates).
G Footpath sign points down Kincaple Den, the road to Guard Bridge marked on Roy´s map of 1755.
H Pale grey sandstone was taken from the deep quarry in the wood to St Andrews. Stone for Balmerino Abbey is reputed to have been taken overland in the 14th century.
J It was claimed that the wrong people were held responsible for the Archbishop´s murder in 1679, and the stone commemorates those who could have been unjustly executed.

This takes us round the forested rim of a bowl containing several farms. To avoid too much walking in forest we take a loop which gives dramatic views over the Tay and the North Fife hills. Wild roe deer are common and the walk also passes a pioneer red deer farm.

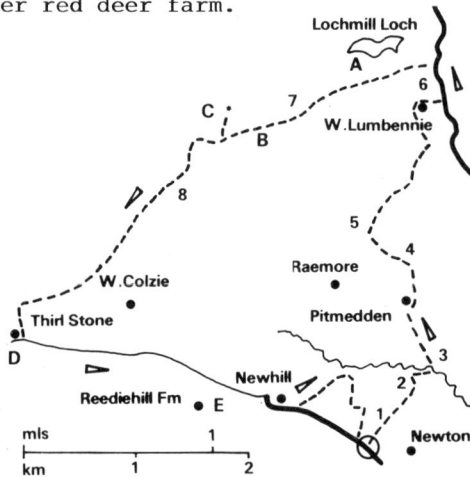

1 GR 222 129. Park off road at south eastern corner of forest. Walk north west along public road to a rough layby and follow narrow winding path up through trees. Where a wheel track comes in from the right, cross broken wall and continue along track northeastwards. You cross a broad ride and go straight on.

2 At the edge of the wood turn left along vehicle track and pass round cottage on your right along a tarmac road above the burn.

3 Turn back left after the bridge, to Pitmedden Farm, through the farmstead and look for a gate near the corner of the forest, left. Do not pass through the gate unless you wish to take a short cut to a point later in the walk, but continue half right over a ridge to a cattle grid with wooden bars above. Head for corner of forest,left.

4 The modern forest road has been bulldozed over the old road on the right which you can clamber down to. Continue until a low place with a crag ahead and turn right between larch, left, and spruce, right, to the farm/forest road.

5 At the cattle grid and wicket gate, head for right corner of isolated wood (any detour for cattle is best to the left). Another cattle grid round the end of the wood, then head for Wester Lumbennie farmstead and turn right for public road.

6 Turn left and left again at the top of the ridge. You will shortly see Lochmill Loch below you on the right.

7 After the power lines ignore forest road to the left and continue ahead to Seven Gates (six in the forest, the seventh leads into a field). Turn right for a few yards for a view of the Tay and return. Now take the wheel track to the right, outside the corner of the field, and follow along edge of wood.

8 After the road enters the trees, turn left at a junction and emerge onto the main Auchtermuchty-Abernethie forest road. Turn half left (ignore the grassy track into the trees) and keep straight on as far as the entrance to Reedie Hill deer farm, right. Past Newhill house, take a woodland track after the burn; it climbs away from the burn above a steep cliff. Stay inside the wood when you come to the fence and climb to the right, then left at the corner. Follow forest track down to the tarmac road and turn left to start.

A From here Lindores Loch, Ormiston, Lindores and Glenduckie Hills, followed by Norman's Law, stand out as a range through North Fife, parallel to the Tay shore. The loch itself has been raised by a dam but appears to have been excavated by ice from the Tay valley.
B The variety of pebbles in the forest road suggest lengthy transport by glaciers and rivers. Granites, schists and jaspers are particularly noticeable on a wet day. The bed rock alongside the track is of Lower Red Sandstone lava with large gas cavities.
C From the diversion you can see Moncrieff and Kinnoul Hills, but most of Perth is concealed. A number of self-sown spruce have found a foothold in the lava cliff.
D At the west corner of the junction is a stone a metre square with a circular recess. A 'thirl stone' is marked here, at the meeting point of the county boundaries of Perth, Kinross and Fife.
E One of the pioneers of deer farming in Scotland is a former veterinary surgeon. Venison and recipes for cooking it are available from the farmhouse and also at Over Rankeillour Farm on the A91, east of Bow of Fife. Note the high fences and the covered yard for winter shelter.

Walk 35   BLACK LOCH   3 miles (4.8 km)

A short forest walk with scope for further exploration round an attractive minor valley in the hills south of Lindores.

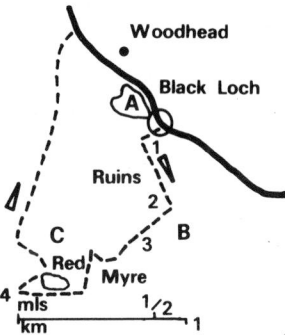

1 GR 263 148. Space for a car at Auchtermuchty end of Black Loch. Step across burn leading out of loch and along left side of fence up the edge of the field to a ruined cottage. Round end of fence and through gate to hillside. Turn left.
2 Pass by a second ruin, and on to the next corner. Turn right around plantation, through gate and on to forest gate.
3 Ignore grass track to the left; go through broom to new forest road and cross to grassy ride, half left, then through to rejoin the same road. Turn right when water is seen ahead, turn left and then right at next junction, along south shore of the small loch.
4 At next broad triangular junction, turn right along north shore to next T junction and turn left. After a few yards take a gate, left, leading out onto the hillside.Turn right, down to the road and right again to start.

A The loch is rapidly being filled in with sediment and an advancing fringe of reeds. Layers of mud at the bottom have been cored down to 11,000 BP, and upper horizons include the Roman occupation. Pollen analysis suggests a contemporary lapse of cultivation.
B The ruined cottage lies on the hill route from Kirkcaldy to Newburgh in use before 1805. Opposite is Green Law, encountered on Walk 36.
C The long axes of Red Myre, Black Loch and Lindores Loch are roughly parallel, consistent with a flow of ice from the west or northwest. Red Myre is notable as a breeding place for blackheaded gulls, but pochard, goldeneye and tufted ducks are also seen. As the hide on the north shore and the numerous bat nesting boxes show, it is an area of scientific interest. Please disturb the birds as little as possible.

A gradual climb along an historic track over to the beautiful Lindores Loch, returning by another hill track over and down to Monimail.

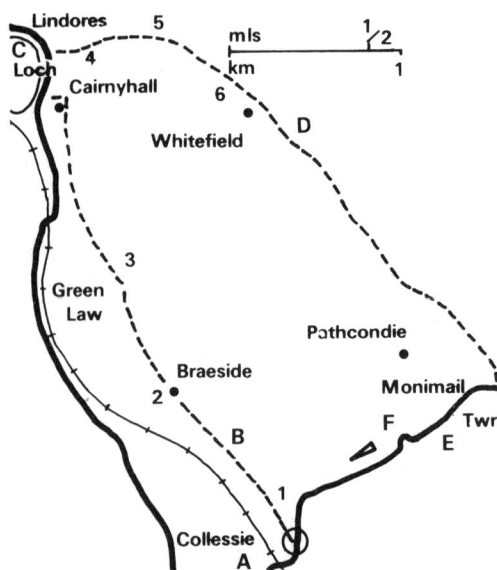

1 GR 286 134. Start north of Collessie church where the road to Monimail crosses the Den Burn, and climb up along the terrace way past a ruined cottage to Braeside steading.
2 Through the buildings and keep to the farm wheeltracks past two gates. Climb the knoll on the left, Green Law, with scattered Scots pines and return to corner of field.
3 Cross to western edge of next field and head for the farm track beyond. Follow this along the contour to Cairneyhall farm. Turn left beyond buildings to road.
4 After anglers' pier take track to the right in front of renovated cottages. Where it crosses a ditch the track continues along the edge of a field.
5 Ignore left turn to ruined cottage and continue right, keeping fence on your left.
6 Track merges with one up from Dunbog. Continue to the right over the col past the ruins of Whitefield farm and down to Monimail. Turn right along public road to start.

A Collessie was bypassed by the present A91 in 1805, and the former Trafalgar Inn stands at the junction.
B The hill track is probably that by which the monks of Lindores carried peat from near Ladybank to their abbey. It was only after 1800 that the valley bottom was drained and it was possible to construct a lower road, and later a railway.
C At the far end of Lindores Loch is Ormiston Hill, visited on Walk 39; the steps formed by the successive lava flows can be clearly seen.
D This route over an exposed col is typical of early roads where directness and good natural drainage were more important than gradient.
E Monimail Tower was part of Archbishop Hamilton's residence in the mid-16th century and now a wine and garden produce cooperative.
F In 1828 the owner of Melville House was anxious to remove this cottage, occupied by an obstinate weaver, to straighten the road. As you can see, the weaver won.

Walk 37   LETHAM TO DUNBOG HILL   4.5 miles (7.2 km)

One of the old routes over the North Fife hills from the
Howe of Fife, using a long narrow col, possibly of glacial
origin. Fine views across the Dunbog valley, to Lindores
Hill and Norman's Law. We return by a parallel col to
Monimail with its historic buildings and associations.

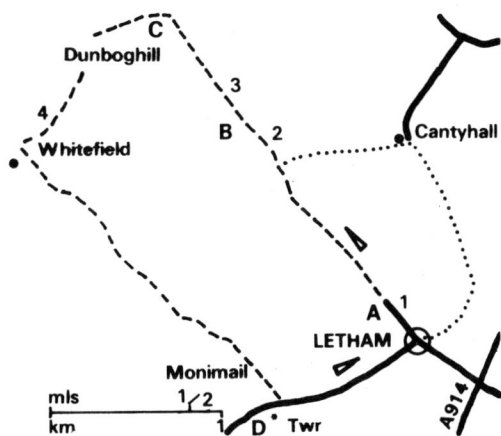

1 GR 307 144. Go up the
main street and through
the wood to a track
along the edge of a
field. Keep straight on
up to corner of fence by
wood. Turn right and
left through wicket
gate.
2 Follow track along
ditch or take right fork
over the knoll to reach
far corner of the part
wooded enclosure at a
rough stile. Walk along
fence to next gate.

3 If there are stock to be avoided, turn left along fence and
climb up to the plantation on the skyline, left. Otherwise
continue along previous line to next fence and turn up left
along rough wheel track to feed area at Dunboghill.
4 Descend along well marked farm road to where it turns to go
down to Dunbog. Here turn left through a gate onto a grassy
wheel track past the ruined Whitefield farmstead. Continue
down to Monimail past the quarry and turn left to start.

A Before the building of the precursor of the A914 in
Letham was an important crossroads village, with a livestock
market, and the road to the east past the farmhouse and
Cantyhall to rejoin our route is recommended.
B Like the lochs to the west noted in Walk 35 the col shows a
northwesterly trend and can be followed right over to Dunbog.
C Between Dunbog and Lindores a route round the lower ground
avoided the reed filled depressions now bypassed by the A913,
and two branches from this detour converged at the Whitefield
col, an exposed place for a farmhouse.
D Set back from the road is Monimail Tower (see Wk 36).

Walk 38   LADYBANK AND DAFTMILL   6 miles (9.6 km)

The broad valley of the River Eden, the Howe of Fife, is here
strewn with deposits of sand and gravel washed out from the
edges of retreating ice sheets. While generally flat, the
minor hollows, knolls and variations in soil give a pleasing
variety of vegetation, especially types of woodland.

Daftmill Fm
Twr
Rankeillour
Mains
7
Pitlair
G
F
E
8
6
5
H
Peterhead
Annsmuir
D
4
Golf Cse
J
9
Sweethome
10
The Wilderness
3 C
Ramornie
Rly
Stn
A
2 B
mls
½
LADYBANK
km
1

1 GR 306 096. At the station car park turn left along path beside wall and pass under railway bridge. At the road junction cross the B9129 and, if the season permits, go between the pillars with slender conical tops and across field to isolated copse of pines. If crops may be damaged, turn up street to left and take track on right.

2 Follow the track at the north of the copse until a yew tree on the right, at the corner of rough ground. Turn back sharp left and then right along edge of wood.

3 Continue along old drive to Sweethome exit. Walk with due care across railway and turn right for Peterhead.

4 Through gate past farmstead and swing to right over bridge. Turn left at top and follow track to wood. Turn right along grass track at field edge and left at corner.

5 Pass to left of Rankeillour Mains buildings with clock, and cross stone bridge. Carry on through the woodland to the road by a lodge and turn right.

6 Before next bridge turn up by sign ´Pitlair´, but take right hand road along the burn.

7 At Daftmill Farm turn left along the wall and pass a cottage with dormers on your right. Head for white tower.

8 At corner of wood go left of water installation into the wood and follow grass track beyond piggery and cross to the right to join a recent forest road. Turn left and emerge at corner of golf course.

9 At next corner, pick up path to right between edge of wood and golf course, or parallel path just inside wood. At end head for white lamp post, where you can cross the railway.

10 Walk between golf car park and contractor´s yard, and carry on alongside railway to start.

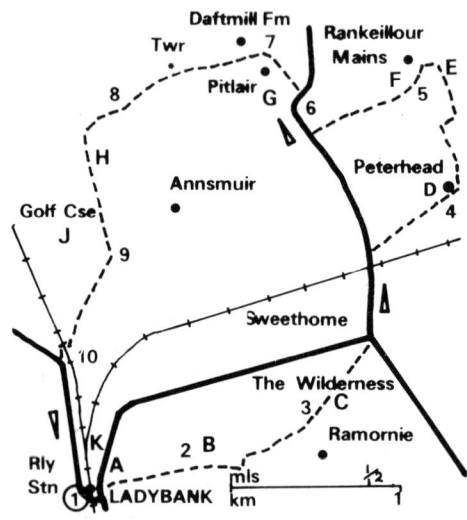

A A plaque on the Masonic Hall records an earlier M.P. for East Fife who often spoke here.

B Good view of Cults Hill (see Walk 13). The River Eden crosses the almost level ground and the main road to Cupar follows a string of villages along the lower slopes.

C The road winds between birch scrub, grassy heath and reed-filled hollows and suggests the ´wilderness´ landscape of the Howe before improvement and the 1797 roads.

D Remains of a waterwheel at the side of the building, fed by a lade from the burn -- a rare opportunity to get a head of water in this almost flat area.

E A typical Fife doocot of the lectern design, with a low side door for collecting the eggs, squabs and mature birds.

F A fine range of buildings with high doors for carriages. The bridge bears the date 1802.

G Pitlair is a recent house with ogee slate turrets and dormers, matched in style by the water tower with windpump.

H The modern plantations replace former generations of planting recorded over 300 years ago on this light sandy land. A former camp is now used for a modern leisure caravan site, and the high walls to the south would have offered protection from stray bullets when used as a range.

J The golf course has made good use of the natural undulations typical of this landscape.

A gradual climb to an impressive viewpoint looking over Newburgh, Dundee and the Tay valley. The north side of the hill shows the successive steps or 'traps' formed by upturned edges of southward dipping lava flows.

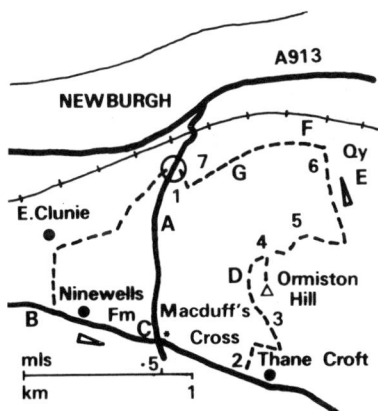

1 GR 228 178. There is space for a car on the housing estate road. Walk to rear of farm buildings and through iron wicket gate along farm track. The way is clear to Easter Clunie and there are hard roads beyond.

2 Half way between Whinnybank and Thane Croft turn up left towards the quarry and right at the top, up a grassy track. Turn left at fence and continue parallel until end of long field on your right.

3 Cross or go round field towards gorse covered cliff and along fence. A diversion north is necessary to reach a gateway and then head for the ladder stile.

4 Over stile and through wicket gate, along wall till grass track up to the left and scramble over rampart to cairn at the summit. Return by same route and turn right, keeping enclosure on your right.

5 At a knoll with gorse and piles of stones, turn right between the fence and the top of a low cliff, down to another fence at the upper edge of a row of fields. Turn left and where a hill fence interrupts the path, go through one gate and back through the next.

6 At corner post of last field bear left across shallow bowl to meet path by quarry notice. Follow path left along foot of crags.

7 At the wicket gate either walk down field past cottage and turn left to start, or climb over to uphill side of fence and through gateway by water filter station (square brick building).

A The steep road was maintained by tolls charged at Pitcairlie (237 141) but would have been abandoned by coach traffic as soon as the road round Hatton Hill was completed.

B Coaches bound for Perth from Auchtermuchty would pass Ninewells Farm and Broomfield. The latter section is in danger of closure as a right of way.

C Only the plinth of Macduff's Cross remains. Traditionally a sanctuary for members of the clan.

D The fort is enclosed by the single rampart, up to 10 feet thick and has been dated as Early Iron Age.

E A more complex fort, containing early Christian remains has been almost entirely destroyed by quarrying.

F A closer view on the left of the edge of a lava flow. Such layers formed part of an arch which extended over the site of the modern Tay. The Sidlaw Hills are their counterparts on the north slope.

G A fine view over Newburgh here, with the old quays at which goods were transferred to barges to be taken up to Perth. The site being developed is that of the recently demolished linoleum works.

A wild craggy hill with an iron age fort, from which we descend through woodland and by a further hill track to the A913. A disused railway embankment, full of wildlife, brings us back to the Glenduckie road junction near the old Dunbog church.

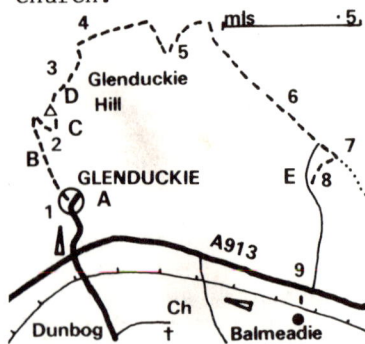

1 GR 282 188. Park opposite large stone at entrance to Glenduckie village, which you leave on your right as you climb past old quarry buildings up a restored forest road.

2 Where there is a zigzag near the top, bear right and scramble up to the ridge above. Continue up left across rampart of hill fort and up to summit.

3 Descend to the north east down the ridge to where the metalled forest road ends by a fence. A stile by a gate leads to a track through a plantation (take care not to damage young trees). The track passes round the north side of a wooded knoll, after which you will see a wooden gate into a field, left.

4 Walk down the field edge to just above the lower corner of the wood, where a tractor road leads through trees, right.

5 Look for a junction with a sharp turning left. This leads across a field to a pair of gates. Cross burn and walk uphill along wall opposite to wood. Turn right in wood.

6 Pass four cottages and you descend to an open area with a gate, right, to Ayton Hill, and a group of buildings.

7 Continue to an isolated square brick building with large sliding doors at the rear and look behind it for a grassy track past a ruined octagonal building. (If this way is difficult, the original road past the front of the first building will lead you down to the main road).

8 The grassy track is overgrown at one point by rhododendrons. Pass round these to the left and descend to the gravel road where you turn left and walk down to road.

9 Turn right and then left where there is a sign to Balmeadie and follow the railway embankment past the isolated Dunbog church, left, to a gap where the bridge has been removed. The old church stands nearby. Descend to the village road and turn north to cross the main road and return to the start.

A Like Letham in Walk 37, Glenduckie was on an important hillside road before it was bypassed by what is now the A913. Two mill ponds can be seen and an embankment supports stoneware pipes to the mill. The upper pond is dry, the lower one grows some fine reedmace and a pretty water garden has been made at the outflow. Ruined doocot by cottages.

B A fine view, left, over Tay islands and port of Newburgh.

C The hill fort is in a commanding position looking over the sweeping valley through Dunbog. Associated with it is a larger enclosure for stock and several hut circles.

D Great care is needed not to damage young trees.

E A large house stood overlooking the artificial pool to the southeast and above there are many features of well planned pleasure grounds, including magnificent daffodils in April.

Formed of dark igneous rocks of Old Red Sandstone age, these hills are the remains of an arch which once reached over to the Sidlaw Hills behind Dundee, and the strata are thus inclined to the south. With heathers, mat grass and bare rock this is one of the wildest places in northern Fife with fine views along the Tay. Defensive ramparts can clearly be seen near the top. The return route includes a hillside road typical of those that carried the traveller on firm ground above the marshes of a post-glacial valley floor. Robert Baillie of Luthrie was responsible for organising many of the late 18th century road improvements.

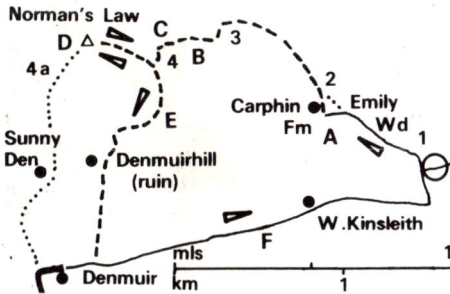

1 GR 325 193. At the gate to Carphin turn right and follow the road north. At the end of Emily Wood either cross the field to the right along a grassy track or go through the farmstead.
2 Cross cattle grids and walk up along the hollow. When the wheel tracks turn left keep straight on towards oaks at corner of pine wood.

3 Follow lower path through wood to reach wooden gate. Keep right of rocky knoll along slope to northern edge of second wood of scots pine. Pass through wicket gate.
4 Walk left to foot of spur and climb to the summit via two cairns. Return by same route to foot of spur and head in same direction (south) to a steel gate in a fence. A wheel track will take you down to the Denmuir-Luthrie road.
4a Grazing cattle may be avoided by descending from the summit to the west to the hillside parallel to the wood. Aim for separate group of pines near corner of fence where there is a gate. Pick cattle tracks down to gate between two bungalows near power line posts (marked ´Denmuir House´). Hard road leads to Denmuir farmstead. Turn left to start

A A doocot with crowstep gables stands in the field to the left. The tenant once had to allow the landlord´s pigeons to eat up his crops so that the landlord could have fresh meat.
B Two species of heather here - bell and ling - with orange hawkweed. Self sown birch is colonising lightly grazed slope.
C The Scots pine to the south with open floor and blaeberries contrasts with the dense sitka spruce.
D The summit. Note the ridge formed by the inner defences to this hill settlement. One wall is 12 ft thick and may be of post-Roman date. Perth is just round the bend of the Tay beyond Kinnoull Hill, but Dundee and St Andrews are clearly seen. The twin volcanic necks of the Lomonds mark the southern skyline and in the foreground there are the sweeping curves of valleys broadened by overflowing icelobes, now followed by the late 18th century roads.
E Cattle are grazed here in summer and may be avoided by taking the alternative route to the west of the summit.
F The green lane contains many wild flowers sprayed out elsewhere, such as scabious and knapweed.

From the attractive ridge road there are views over the whole Eden estuary and the valley of the Motray Water. Sharp contrasts in building materials and old quarry routes add further interest. Easy walking.

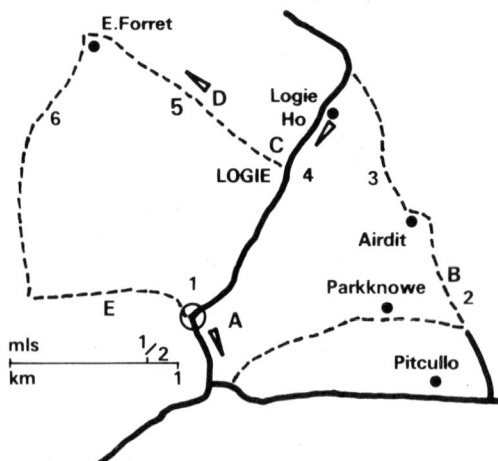

1 GR 404 203. Park by the metal gate and head south to the junction before the cottage. Turn left and look for a gap in the wall where the road curves round to the right. Cross left to the hedge line and follow down through the farmstead to a belt of trees on your left.

2 A hollow way to the east of the trees marks the old road, but in summer a way through the trees may be preferable. Keep within belt till it curves sharply to the left opposite a rocky knoll on your right, and at the entrance to Airdit cottage turn right up gravel track.

3 Continue past cottage at junction to main road and turn sharp left past Logie House.

4 At Logie village turn right between former chapel, now a community hall, and the pink stone schoolhouse, left. Carry on past sign Wester Logie Farm and white cottage, descending along the flank of Forret Hill.

5 At the wood you will see Easter Forret farm ahead. Turn left after the farmhouse through a gate and head for a second gate across the corner of the field. Continue to the right on the level, along lower side of fence around the hill.

6 Opposite Wester Forret (on the main road), change to uphill side of wall to reach terrace way with farm track down past quarry. Through gateway to grassy wheel track between walls up the slope ahead. Turn left at the crossroads and a similar track leads you back to the start.

A A view across Leuchars airfield down the main runway, with Guardbridge paper mill to the right.

B The road is a possible route by which stone could be taken from quarries near Strathkinness to Balmerino Abbey, although a more easterly route has been suggested. The 16th century tower house of Pitcullo was restored in 1971.

C Note the use of the hard pink stone of Lucklaw Hill in the walls and some of the houses. Quoins and window dressings are in sandstone.

D Ahead in the valley is the village of Kilmany with its simple white church. The continuation of the old railway used in Walk 46 can be clearly seen. Also the old Kilmany-Gauldry road by which travellers up to 1800 reached the Woodhaven ferry to Dundee.

E These grassy tracks are almost untouched by modern farming methods and provide a rich habitat for wild flowers, birds and butterflies.

An easy walk round the slopes of a hill which commands views over the whole of eastern Fife, particularly the Motray valley and Tentsmuir.

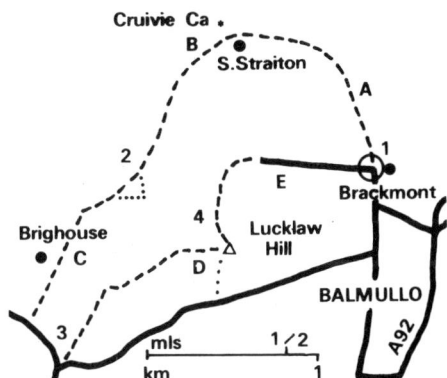

Cruivie Ca .
B
S.Straiton
A
2
E
Brackmont
4
Brighouse
C
Lucklaw
Hill
D
BALMULLO
3
mls   1/2
km   1
A92

1 GR 427 221. Be prepared to park a car some distance from the start, for farm traffic must not be obstructed. Descend along the good road leading round to South Straiton. After this it becomes a rough track and winds up the west slopes of Straiton Hill. Near the wood the end of the road has been fenced off and it is necessary to go along the field edge beyond.

2 Where there is a half gate and rails on your left at the corner of the wood, head across field, if crops permit, towards a group of conifers under powerlines to the right, otherwise follow round the edge of the field. Beyond, you come to a grassy track which meets a gravelled road. Turn left, and left again at the public road.

3 Through gate and along left side of wall until, after a corner, there is a gateway where the wall is offset. Move to the right side and head for a clump of trees across the field, following a tractor wheel track. An iron wicket gate in the corner leads onto the top of Lucklaw Hill. An alternative route is shown if livestock need to be left undisturbed: along the road, through gate on left and up the field fence nearest to the quarry

4 Return from the summit by a wicket gate in the woodland fence to the north west. From here there are several minor tracks through bracken, blaeberry and birch scrub, but keep going downhill and you will reach the main woodland road. Turn right past some cottages and down hard road to start.

A In the Motray valley ahead and to the right are the curious landforms associated with a retreating ice lobe: outwash gravels, kames or boulder ridges. Beyond North Straiton Farm a plateau has been attributed to the silting up of a marginal lake trapped between the ice and the hillside.

B Access to Cruivie Castle is to the left of the main buildings and round the open barn.

C An interesting developmentof a farmstead to provide dwellings at Brighouse.

D A variety of vegetation to the west of the hill, with rushy hollows, scrub woodland and bracken, leading up to an almost pure expanse of blaeberry at the summit. An excellent view over the whole of Tentsmuir, Leuchars airfield, the Eden estuary and St Andrews with its golf course.

E On the eastern slope of Lucklaw Hill are grown specialised crops such as strawberries. Many of the homes are occupied by service personnel and others who have come to reconcile a beautiful position with a certain level ofnoise.

After climbing a wild rocky knoll with good views there is the opportunity of a scramble up to the north side of Norman's Law (see Walk 41), but this is optional, since we return to the road and descend to the Tay shore. An old church set in woods and a good leg stretch back complete this easy walk.

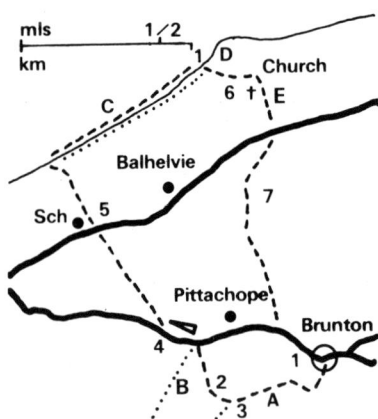

1 GR 317 208. If there is no car space the start could be west of Pittachope Farm. Over metal gate and across small field to corner of wood. Climb narrow track up the ridge to the summit and descend to fence beyond.

2 If omitting Norman's Law the orthodox route takes you along the fence to the road.

3 Over fence at corner of wood and head for the summit of the Law. It is easiest to climb the east (lefthand) end. Return to road.

4 A few yards west along the road turn right through gate and along edge of field to wicket gate onto lower road opposite disused school house.

5 Route should go through the wooded den but overgrown at present, so go down alongside fence to shore and turn right.

6 Turn up behind fishing bothy through wood to W.Flisk church, then up to the road. Take track opposite in wood.

7 At the edge of the wood there is no defined track, but head south for the top of the slope, where a gate leads on to a farm track to Pittachope Farm. The track turns right but the way is overgrown ahead, so we must go along the edge of the field to the right of the fence to reach the road, and turn left to start.

A Undisturbed spots such as this, with its growth of mosses, lichens, grasses and heathers, are becoming rare in Fife, and part of this hillside is protected for scientific study.

B The lava crags along the track up to Norman's Law are particularly rich in flower species.

C The deep channel is close inshore, and is taken by small tankers and freighters at high tide going up to the quays of Perth. The overhanging trees may make the shore difficult and you must be prepared to follow the top edge of the bank.

D Sweep net fishing for sea trout and salmon is a traditional source of income, although the dearth of salmon in recent years has reduced the numbers of fishermen. The rights along the Tay have been protected by statutes from the 15th century.

E In the churchyard many of the headstones are of interest, particularly those indicating the craft of the deceased.

Walk 45   MOUNTQUHANIE TO BIRKHILL   5 Miles   (8 km)

Through the attractive woodland of the North Fife hills and down to the Tay shore where there are some fine specimen trees. The walk overlooks the shallow post-glacial trough occupied by the Motray and followed by the old railway.

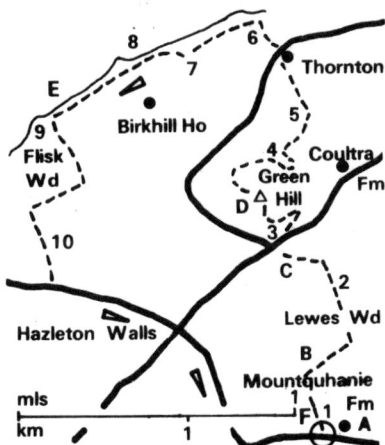

1 GR 347 214. Start just to the east of the cottages and walk up farm road. After first wood, at filled in pond on left, turn right and through plantation with deer gates and stiles.
2 Continue past an open space on your right, Tay Mount, and go into wood along ride ahead. After first belt of spruce turn left into larch and descend to road at corner of field.
3 Climb woodland track opposite to the right which, after a sharp turn left, winds up to excavated cairn at the summit. Bear left to the corner of a spruce plantation on the north slope and descend to a track along to the right.
4 At an open area with a filled in pond on your left, go round and follow a power line through the wood for a few yards, then turn up bank into wood up to open stand of larch.
5 Where the track levels out, go down left to field and along track to right. Follow next fence downhill to road. Turn right to farm and left into field, to far left corner.
6 Cross ditch and enter wood, keeping to left of deep ditch, then straight down through the trees to a horizontal track. Turn left. At waymark post with two arrows, go left.
7 After crossing three footbridges and passing some mature hardwood trees see ahead a gate into a private garden. Go back to a clearing by an old yew tree and turn downhill past a spreading beech tree and take the lower path to the left.
8 At a broad cleared strip running down from the house, turn right through a tunnel in rhododendrons to above the shore.
9 At a promontory on the shore by Birkhill fishing lodge, a track leads up left through the woods by Corbies Den. Go right with the track to pass a sawmill. Turn left.
10 At bend to the right, go straight on through wood along grassy track, and where it emerges go straight up the field (usually under raspberries) up to a gate onto the road and turn left. Walk on to cross roads at Hazleton Walls and go straight on to to start.

A The big farm building by the road displays the local dark volcanic rock, squared off with great labour. The quoins are of sandstone as is usual in all Fife cottages.
B You may recognise cottage garden 'escapes', such as the Cotoneaster on the opposite wall and leopard's bane.
C The open larch woodland encourages a good cover of grasses, fungi, ferns, blueberries and wild raspberries.
D The cairn was excavated around 1900 when cists with food vessels were found. Unfortunately this was before modern archaeological methods and much evidence was destroyed.
E For the practice of salmon fishing, see Walk 44 Note C.
F Mountquhanie Castle, A 16th century tower house, was romantically converted to a ruin and planted with ivy when the later house was built in the 1830s.

Walk 46   KILMANY - GAULDRY - STIRTON   6.5 miles (10.5 km)

We set off along what was the main road from Edinburgh to Aberdeen as it climbs the North Fife ridges, cross farmland with sweeping views and return along a disused railway to the attractive village of Kilmany. Easy gradients but some rough vegetation.

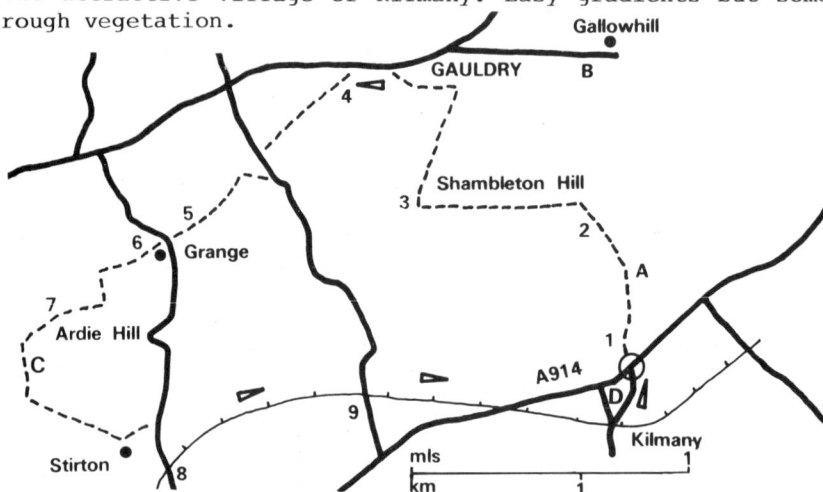

Gallowhill

GAULDRY   B

4

Shambleton Hill

3

2

5

6   Grange

A

7

Ardie Hill

1

C

A914

D

9

Kilmany

Stirton

8

mls

km

1 GR 388 220. Leave the busy A914 and head north up the brae, over the slope and across a burn, keeping left along a strip of woodland. The old road now lies to your left.
2 On entering the main wood step into the hollow way on the left along a line of small beech trees and then take the path along the slope through the trees to the left.
3 At end of woods, keep on round to the right and head for the east end of Gauldry. A narrow path along a hedge, right, becomes a rough wheel track. Turn left round a new house at the corner and along the rear of the row of houses to Balgove Road at a range of stone farm buildings. Turn left and reach main road via Hays Road. Turn left.
4 At end of village there is a garage building. Turn left and go to the right of this along a grassy strip down the slope, passing through a patch of broom, to the next road. Turn left and then back right, up a farm track to resume the same line, passing an isolated ash tree.
5 Along edge of field, over steps in wall and through gate.
6 Pass farmhouse on your left and walk through farmstead up right side of burn. Continue to next cross fence and turn left up wide grassy strip to wood.
7 Follow edge of wood uphill and round to the left until derelict fence line connecting to upper wood. Turn left at wood and follow grass track. Turn left down to Stirton.
8 Turn right along road and go under old railway bridge. Turn right and scramble up embankment. Turn right again.
9 As this bridge has been removed, you will have to scramble down and up the other side of the road, but it is then a straight through walk past old platform of Kilmany station to the village. Right at school and past church to start.

A Heavy traffic has scoured a hollow way over the shoulder of the hill. This was one of the earliest roads to be shown on a map of Fife (Dorret 1750).
B East of Gauldry is Gallow Hill, whence the name derives.
C The railway to be followed later can be seen below along the floor of the valley beyond Stirton Farm. The Motray Water is a ´misfit´ in that it follows a trough created by a more powerful agency, ice, of which the deposits south of Wormit are evidence.
D The church has a domestic look, built as rectory 1768.

A gentle climb to the undulating slopes above the Tay shore.
A varied landscape with several types of woodland, ending at
the old port of Balmerino near the ruined abbey. We return
close to the shore with views across to Dundee.

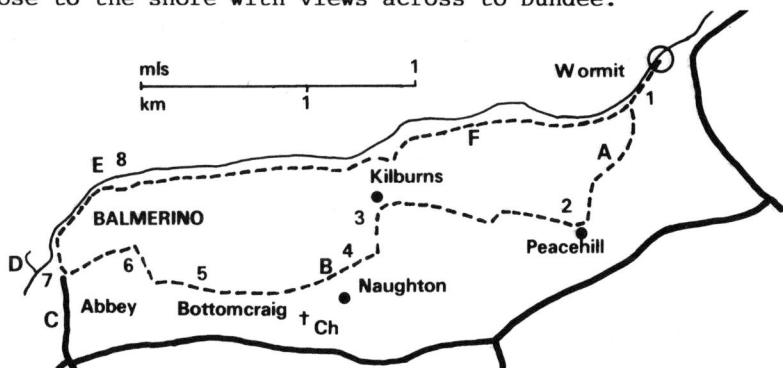

1 GR 392 259. From car park, walk above shore wall to an
opening in the fence, turn left and up farm track to
Peacehill Farm.
2 Turn right past farmhouse and then between the cottages,
following the road to Kilburn.
3 Through farmstead and turn up left along belt of trees.
Left and right to top of ridge.
4 Descend to the right between woods and where the road
turns left follow it round past timber farm building with
tin roof to a double fenced farm road to Bottomcraig. The
way is straight on, but you may wish to take a loop round to
the left to visit the church and return.
5 Path enters wood then down a slope to a dilapidated
bridge, to be crossed with care. At the field turn left
along the burn to the road and turn right.
6 At cypress hedge in Kirkton turn left past stone buildings
and then left at next junction to pass churchyard.
7 Turn right past NEFDC signpost 'to Wormit' and follow
shore path round.
8 Just after industrial buildings at Nether Kirkton bear
right, up grassy track to follow edge of field. The track
continues either at the top of the cliff or along the slope
back to the start. There is a steep sided den at 377 256,
after the second shelter belt, but you can zigzag down
without much difficulty.

A This was the coach road from Edinburgh over to the
Woodhaven ferry (Walk 48). The present B946 was not built
until 1804.
B Naughton Castle, through the trees,is of the 12th century
and beyond is a fine 18th century house.
C Balmerino Abbey (NTS) was a Cistercian foundation (1227).
The original stone is believed to have come from a nearby
quarry, but stone for repairs has been attributed to Nydie.
D A ruined jetty, left, served coal importing and grain
exporting ships. Yarn for the cottage weavers also came in
from Dundee and there was a passenger service.
E This is marked as a 'boiling house' (for whale blubber) on
older maps and was later used for packing scallops. Piles of
shells can be seen below the path to the east. On the
foreshore agates may be found (concentric infilling of lava
gas cavities).
F Good views here of the two bridges, with the ports of
Woodhaven and Newport beyond, and across to Dundee.

Walk 48   WOODHAVEN AND NEWTON HILL   5.5 miles (8.8 km)

A lobe of ice overflowing from the Tay valley has left a
curious jumble of debris south of Newport. Our walk crosses
and returns over this landscape, visiting the historic ferry
port of Woodhaven by following a grass covered turnpike
road.

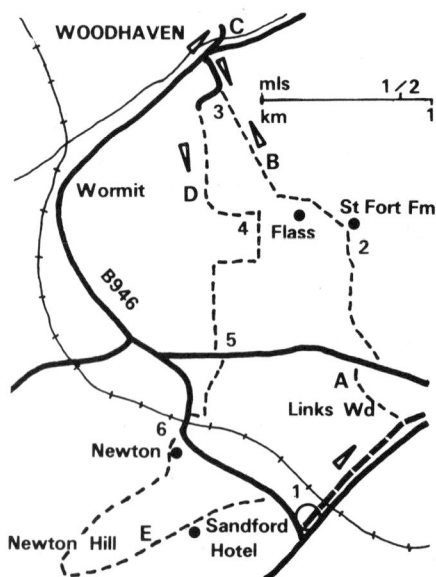

1 GR 410 241. A car may be
parked in the old lower road
near the railway. Continue
under the railway bridge and
on to the edge of West Links
Wood. Near where the tarmac
finishes, a ride leads into
the wood, left. At the other
end a right fork leads you
onto a road. Turn right, then
left at sign.
2 Turn left at the farm
buildings and just past the
second farmstead, Flass, take
a woodland track by wooden
huts on the right. Follow
this to the corner, where
there is an easy place over
the wall. Walk straight down
towards houses.
3 Turn left into Crosshill
Terrace and then right, down Flass Road. At main road turn
right for a few yards and then fork left, down to Woodhaven
pack house and pier. Return by same route as far as junction
with Ericht Road, where you carry on up a short access road
to the side of Flass Cottage and then up a grassy wheel
track. Follow this to top of ridge.
4 Opposite a small building turn down a farm track to the end
of the first field, through a gateway and then turn right on
the level past an old quarry (piles of stones). At the line
of beech trees turn downhill.
5 Near the foot of the fence there is a gate, left, onto the
road. Turn right and take the first gate on your left. Follow
the fence down alongside the gravel pit to a gate into the
pit access road and turn right to main road, then left under
railway bridge. Beware of large lorries turning.
6 Through Newton farmstead and up the hill track to the
right. Where this opens out into a field beyond the last
crags on the left, make your way to the corner of the field
on the ridge, where there is a gate alongside a disused
wicket gate. Follow the track to the line of electricity
poles and then along the upper edge of the field
(avoiding gorse scrub) to a wicket gate at the corner onto
the road. Turn right to start.

A The undulations of the ground inside Links Wood are only
extensions of the gravelly ridges being quarried to the west.
The name, as for similar terrain on gravel and sand, is of
course, what we associate with the nearby sport of golf.
B The owner of St Fort was concerned in 1792 about the
steepness of the climb from Woodhaven, and set out the more
winding route to the west by which we shall return.
C The old pack house on the left was built in 1799, as the
plaque indicates, by the turnpike trustees to store goods
awaiting shipment. As a ferry port Woodhaven was eclipsed by

its rival, Newport, by 1821. A recent use of the pack house (now a joinery workshop) was as a Norwegian Flying boat (Catalinas) station; a plaque records a visit by King Haakon.
D Our route corresponds approximately to that taken by the turnpike road before the line of the present A914 was adopted in 1804. An even earlier route was over Newton Hill.
E A fine view along the ridge. The Sandford Hotel is recommended for refreshments.

Walk 49   INVERDOVAT AND KIRKTON   3.5 miles   (5.6 km)

Quietly away from the main traffic roads, here is a varied small scale landscape with wooded crags and old cross country tracks. An extension of the walk northwards to the coast is envisaged.

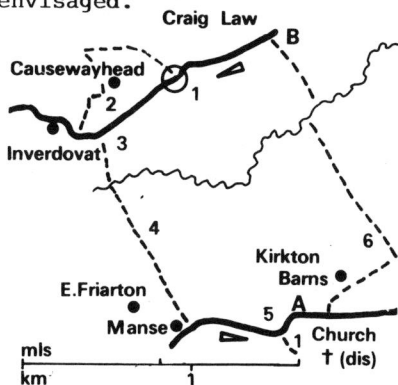

1 GR 441 277. A car may be parked in the old quarry west of the bridge. A grassy track opposite leads into a larch wood and follows the foot of a steep cliff. At the end walk round outside of wood to gateway beyond embankment. Turn left.
2 Past Causewayhead farmstead turn right, pass round wood and to left of cottages on road. Turn left.

3 Over wall before corner of wood, right, and down side of wood. Through gate at lower corner into field and down left hand side of wall to ditch. Cross to remains of wicket gate and head for gate opposite, to the right of the broom covered area. Turn left after gate and then right, up the tree free strip along the power line.
4 At the southern fence turn left to a metal gate and down the slope to pass to left of the manse. Turn left at road.
5 You may wish to visit the church yard. Then continue to farm road, left, to Kirkton Barns. Past the farmstead and turn left past the wood.
6 Follow the straight track north to the Scotscraig Burn and swing to the right as far as the wood. Cross the burn and follow fence line up to road. Turn left to start.

A The Kirkton of the parish of Forgan is all that remains of a village with its own annual fair in the 17th century. In the burial ground there are several examples of craft symbols on headstones, including that of a gardener.
B Start of walk to north shore. Some determination needed.

This may be combined with visits to the ferry terminus at Tayport harbour of the first railway to cross Fife (1848). The site of the Nature Conservancy reserve at Morton Lochs was a shoreline in mesolithic times and great middens of limpets were found there. The whole of Tentsmuir is the result of the accretion of blown sand, much of which was planted with pines in the 1920s. Take field glasses for the hide at Morton Lochs or drive to the car park there later.

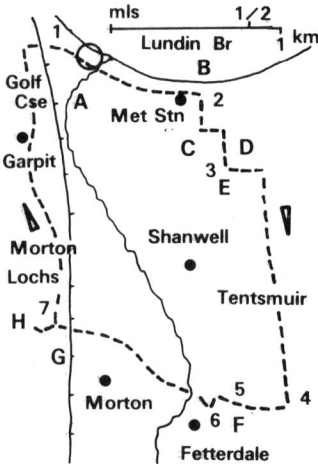

1 GR 467 279. Turn off B945 in Tayport by bus shelter down Maitland St and first right along Nelson St. Past golf course to Lundin Bridge. Park on open ground before bridge. Walk east past meteorological station as far as concrete blocks. Turn inland past wooden barrier.

2 Enter wood at T road junction and on along narrow track. Turn left at next T junction then, after 50 yards, right.

3 At T junction, left along track with heather until clear felled area (1987). Turn right.

4 At rail barrier turn right along hard road. Scrub birch on left, field ahead.

5 After road bears left turn right. Pass wooden bar,turn left (Right turn sign says to Shanwell).

6 At entrance to Fetterdale (Forestry Commission office) turn right and right again at deer fenced plantation. Ignore left fork. Over bridge and on to bird hide (high fence).

7 Return to take path east of lochs (do not enter reserve). Walk north to edge of wood, across field past Garpits Farm, across golf course and return to start.

A The Lundin Burn can be traced on the map, but preferably not on foot, to within a few yards of the main runway. Its long northerly course results from the constant blocking of any easterly outlet by fresh sand dunes. Views across to the old Broughty Ferry train harbour and Broughty Castle (museum). Broad mudflats at low tide with exposed mussel scalps, formerly valued as fish bait, and a variety of wading birds.

B Dunes here show the condition of much of Tentsmuir before the trees.

C Well lit floor under pines carries ferns, raspberries, many mosses and fungi.

D Bell heather, ling, tormentil as on the old heathland.

E Bird box ahead is reminder of value of this area as a biological laboratory.

F Under-storey of rowan beneath pines.

G Railway opened 1848. Train ferry made redundant by first Tay Bridge 1879. Line closed 1966.

H Move quietly in the hide and observe wildfowl. Lagoons have been created by building an earth ridge, shelter also visual cover for shy species.

REFERENCES

BIBLIOGRAPHY

Armstrong, M., Paterson, I.B. and Browne, M.A.E., ´Geology of the Perth and Dundee district´ British Geological Survey H.M.S.O. (1985)

Bennett, G.P., ´The Great Road between Forth and Tay´ Markinch (1983)

Chesher, S., Foster, L. and Hogben, L. ´A Short History of the Villages Charlestown, Limekilns and Pattiesmuir´ Charlestown Community Council (1979)

Cunningham, A.S., ´Lundin Links, Upper and Lower Largo and Leven´ Portobello (1913)

Forsyth, D., In ´Walker´s Britain´ Pan Books/Ordnance Survey (1982)

Forsyth, I.H. and Chisholm, J.I., ´The Geology of East Fife´ Memoirs of the Geological Survey of Great Britain H.M.S.O. (1977)

Haldane, D. and Allan, J.K. ´The Economic Geology of the Fife Coalfields: Area 1 Dunfermline and West Fife´ Memoirs of the Geological Survey of Great Britain (1931)

Hallewell, R., (1) ´Walk Perthshire, 45 Walks in Perth and Kinross District´ Edinburgh (1986)

Hallewell, R., (2) ´Walk Lothian, the Borders and Fife´ Edinburgh (1988)

Jardine, I., ´Seatoun of Largo´ St Andrews (1982)

Lamont-Brown, R., ´Discovering Fife´ Edinburgh (1988)

MacGregor, A.R., ´Fife and Angus Geology´ Edinburgh (1973)

McNeill, C., ´Come in to Cardy´ In Scots Magazine (August 1987)

Scott Bruce, W., ´The Railways of Fife´ Perth (1980)

Silver, O.B., ´The Roads of Fife´ Edinburgh (1987)

Smith, A., ´ The Third Statistical Account of Scotland: The County of Fife´ Edinburgh (1952)

Smith, R.F. and Johnson, N.M., ´From Quarry to Abbey: An Ancient Fife Route´ In Proceedings of the Society of Antiquaries of Scotland 83 (1948-9, 162-167)

Stephen W.M., ´The Binnend Oilworks and the Binn Village´ Research by Adult Education Class in Industrial Archaeology, Fife Education Committee, Kirkcaldy (?1968)

Walker, B. and Ritchie, R., ´Exploring Scotland's Heritage: Fife and Tayside´ Royal Commission on the Ancient and Historic Monuments of Scotland, Edinburgh (1987)

Webster, J.M., ´The History of Carnock, Fife´ London (1938)

Whatley, C.A., ´That Necessary Article: The Salt Industry and its Trade in Fife and Tayside c1570-1850´ Abertay Historical Society Publication No.22 Dundee (1984)

Whittington, G.W. and Jarvis, J.,(1) ´Kilconquhar Loch, Fife: an historical and palynological investigation´ In Proceedings of the Society of Antiquaries of Scotland vol.116 (1986) 413-428

Whittington, G.W., Cundill, P. and Edwards, K.,(2) In Geological Conservation Review on the Quaternary of Scotland vol.37 Nature Conservancy Council (1989, in press)

Willshire, B. and Hunter, D., ´Stones: A guide to Some Remarkable Eighteenth Century Gravestones´ Edinburgh (1978)

Wood, W., ´The East Neuk of Fife´ Edinburgh (1887)

USEFUL ADDRESSES

Dunfermline District Council, Planning Dept, 3 New Row, Dunfermline

Kirkcaldy District Council, Director of Planning, Town House, Kirkcaldy

North East Fife District Council, Director of Planning and Building Control, County Buildings, Cupar

Fife Ranger Service, Lochore Meadows Country Park, Crosshill, Lochgelly

The Ramblers, Scotland, Secretary: William Forsyth, 12 Mosspark Road, Milngavie, Glasgow G62 8NJ

Scottish Rights of Way Society, Secretary: 1 Lutton Place, Edinburgh EH8 9PD

Wemyss Environmental Education Centre, Director: Mrs Ann Watters, Basement Suite, East Wemyss Primary School, East Wemyss.